MY FIRST MILLION With ChatGPT

MY FIRST MILLION With ChatGPT

How to Make Money Online Using Artificial Intelligence.
*Achieve Business Success with a Blueprint to Master
ChatGPT and Profit from Millionaire Prompts.*

Mindscape Artwork Publishing
Mauricio Vasquez

Toronto, Canada

<u>DEDICATION</u>

This book is dedicated to you, the reader, for taking the bold step towards harnessing the power of ChatGPT to shape your future. Your decision to purchase this book is a testament to your willingness to innovate, adapt, and thrive in the rapidly evolving landscape of AI and technology.

We hope this book helps you reach your goals and keeps you motivated to keep growing, learning, and succeeding. By choosing this book, you're already leading the way in the digital age, ready to explore new chances and make your dreams come true.

Scan the QR code to access our book collection.

TABLE OF CONTENTS

Chapter 1
INTRODUCTION

Welcome to your transformative journey with ChatGPT, the gateway to achieving your first million dollars. In a world where ChatGPT has quickly become a cornerstone technology, surpassing user growth records at an unprecedented pace, its potential to revolutionize income generation and business expansion is undeniable.

As of 2023, ChatGPT's meteoric rise to 100 million users underscores its revolutionary impact, surpassing the growth trajectories of Netflix, Twitter, Facebook, and Instagram. This unprecedented adoption signals ChatGPT's potential to redefine how we can make money.

This book guides you to financial success and independence using ChatGPT. This is not just for business owners or entrepreneurs but also for anyone looking to monetize their passions, hobbies or skills using ChatGPT. It reveals how ChatGPT can enhance efficiency, automate tasks, and open alternative paths to generate income for you and your loved ones, acting as more than just a tool but as a crucial ally in reaching your financial aspirations.

This book and ChatGPT invite anyone, regardless of background, profession, or skill level, to explore financial opportunities. It emphasizes that success with ChatGPT hinges on the willingness to engage, learn, and persistently navigate through challenges and opportunities. Resilience and a proactive approach are key to leveraging ChatGPT's capabilities to their full potential for income generation.

The evolving role of words in our work highlights the importance and urgency for us to adapt to AI's capabilities. Where words from our emails, reports or any other written form of communication once signified effort and intelligence, AI now challenges the traditional valuation of these outputs, prompting a reevaluation of work's significance. This technological shift can mean a crisis for some, yet it also opens a door to unprecedented freedom and the opportunity to redefine business and entrepreneurial pursuits. Whether this moment becomes a crisis, or an income-generating opportunity, is entirely in your hands.

By embracing AI, we can delegate the mundane to focus on passion projects, expanding our capabilities beyond natural limits. As we embark on this journey with ChatGPT, let this book be your roadmap to not just surviving but thriving in the AI-enhanced landscape of business and personal growth.

Help Others: Share Your Insight

Should this book unlock new perspectives for you on using technology to enhance your financial well-being or to enrich your professional or personal life in unexpected ways, I invite you to leave a positive review on Amazon. Your review could help others change their lives. Each review is a valuable step in spreading the potential of technology to reshape our future. Thank you for sharing your journey with us and inspiring others to explore their own paths for transformation.

Please scan this QR code to leave your review.

Chapter 2
WHAT IS GENERATIVE ARTIFICIAL INTELLIGENCE?

In the advanced landscape of Artificial Intelligence (AI), Generative AI emerges not merely as an incremental milestone but as a transformative narrative that reconfigures the potential of what AI can achieve. This is not a slight enhancement in AI. Rather, it's revolutionary artificial intelligence technology capable of generating text, images, or other media, using generative models.

Traditional AI excels in data analysis and interpretation, but Generative AI takes a step further. It doesn't just analyze; it creates. This technology is pivotal in generating unique content with real value, particularly in monetizing ChatGPT. From crafting profitable business strategies to developing innovative marketing plans and enhancing income-generating communications, Generative AI reshapes the way we approach money-making solutions. It's not just an assistant; it's a creator, expanding the horizons of human creativity and opening new avenues for financial success.

Generative AI, built on intricate neural networks, transcends simple imitation to master and enhance complex patterns of human behavior. Its influence is vast, reshaping fields like online business, financial planning, and income generation through digital platforms. This isn't just an academic concept; it's a tangible, influential innovation with profound, practical implications in business and entrepreneurship. It can empower you in real time to create lucrative strategies and solutions, marking a significant leap in applying AI to businesses and side hustles.

As the focus shifts to the latest advancements in Natural Language Processing (NLP) and Chatbots, it's vital to recognize that Generative AI forms the core architecture for these sophisticated conversational tools. Particularly in utilizing AI for financial gains and business strategies, Generative AI enhances these platforms by providing not only relevant but also contextually rich and nuanced information and insights. The result is a more advanced application of AI in business. Overlooking the potential of Generative AI means missing out on a wealth of opportunities for innovation and enhanced efficiency.

Chapter 3
WHAT ARE NATURAL LANGUAGE PROCESSING CHATBOTS?

An AI Chatbot is a program within a website or app that uses Machine Learning (ML) and Natural Language Processing (NLP) to interpret inputs and understand the intent behind a request or "prompt" (more on this later in the book). Chatbots can be rule-based with simple use cases or more advanced and able to handle multiple conversations.

The emergence of language models like GPT has transformed the use of conversational AI for business and entrepreneurial success. These advanced Chatbots can now emulate not just human conversational styles but also show exceptional cognitive abilities. They can retrieve information online and generate unique content and insights, which makes them invaluable in creating profitable online strategies, developing innovative business ideas, and enhancing marketing and sales efforts. Their application on the topic of making money with ChatGPT marks a significant leap in exploiting AI for financial gains.

One key thing to know about an AI Chatbot is that it combines ML and NLP to understand what people need and bring the best answers. Some AI Chatbots are better for personal use, like conducting research, and others are best for business use, like featuring a Chatbot on a company's website.

This book focuses on ChatGPT. It uses NLP to understand the context of conversations to provide related and original responses in a human-like conversation, offering multiple use cases for things like answering questions, ideating, and getting inspiration, or generating new content.

As of the book's publication date, the information from this book is current and accurate. The Chatbot industry, however, is dynamic, with constant updates and new entrants. While specifics may evolve, our prompts, core strategies and principles discussed in this book withstand the test of time, offering you a robust framework for navigating this fast-paced landscape.

Chapter 4
BENEFITS OF USING CHATGPT

In today's world, balancing the demands of personal life, professional settings, and business ventures is increasingly challenging. This is where ChatGPT, an advanced conversational AI, comes into play, offering versatile solutions that seamlessly bridge these diverse aspects of life.

ChatGPT's expansive utility in personal, professional, and business contexts stems from its sophisticated AI capabilities, making it an essential asset to attain for a wide range of benefits, including but not limited to:

1. **ENHANCED PERSONAL PRODUCTIVITY:** ChatGPT serves as a digital personal assistant, adept at organizing schedules, suggesting engaging activities, and facilitating the acquisition of new skills. Its utility in personal life management elevates everyday experiences, making them more organized and fulfilling.

2. **REVOLUTIONIZED PROFESSIONAL INTERACTIONS:** In professional environments, ChatGPT is a dynamic enabler. Its proficiency in crafting emails, designing presentations, and summarizing reports revolutionizes standard workflows, bolstering communication efficiency and business productivity.

3. **BUSINESS OPERATIONS TRANSFORMATION:** For entrepreneurs and business owners, ChatGPT stands as a formidable strategic partner. Its capabilities extend from curating compelling marketing materials to insightful market trend analysis and robust customer support, propelling business innovation, customer engagement, and operational efficiency to new heights.

4. **TAILORED SOLUTIONS FOR DIVERSE CONTEXTS:** ChatGPT's bespoke response generation is invaluable across various domains. Whether it's rendering personal development advice, brainstorming innovative business strategies, or fostering professional advancement, its customized approach ensures relevance and effectiveness in every interaction.

5. **FACILITATING LEARNING AND GROWTH:** This book, with ChatGPT's technological prowess, offers a pathway for continuous learning and development. It harmoniously blends personal advisement, professional insights, and strategic business tactics, nurturing growth in all life dimensions.

6. **CATALYZING BUSINESS SUCCESS AND ENTREPRENEURSHIP:** ChatGPT acts as a catalyst on the entrepreneurial journey, offering insights and strategies crucial to starting and scaling businesses. Its deep understanding of market dynamics, consumer behavior, and business planning can significantly enhance decision-making, risk assessment, and innovation in business. From validating business ideas to optimizing strategies for market penetration, ChatGPT becomes an indispensable ally in the quest for business accomplishment and achieving the million-dollar milestone.

In sum, the fusion of ChatGPT's AI expertise with the actionable strategies provided in this book creates a comprehensive toolkit for success. This synergistic combination promises not only to revolutionize professional and business pursuits but also to enrich personal life, fostering a holistic approach to achievement and satisfaction in today's complex world.

Chapter 5
TRANSFORM CHALLENGES INTO TRIUMPHS WITH CHATGPT

In today's rapidly evolving digital era, professionals and business owners across all sectors face unique challenges that can hamper growth and productivity. This chapter dives into some of these challenges, exploring how ChatGPT emerges as a powerful ally, turning obstacles into opportunities for success and innovation.

1. **THE COLD OUTREACH CONUNDRUM:**

   Cold outreach is a familiar struggle for many. Crafting emails or messages that strike the right chord with potential clients is an art form. The process can be time-consuming and fraught with uncertainty. How do you capture attention, convey value, and prompt action, all within a few sentences? The pressure to stand out in a crowded inbox often leads to overthinking and second-guessing, potentially resulting in lost opportunities.

   Here, ChatGPT steps in as a game-changer. By analyzing successful outreach strategies and understanding industry-specific nuances, ChatGPT can swiftly generate compelling, personalized messages. It offers a variety of styles and levels of sophistication, catering to different target audiences and objectives. With ChatGPT, the daunting task of cold outreach or just replying to potential customers' inquiries transforms into a strategic, efficient process, significantly increasing the likelihood of positive responses and fruitful connections.

2. THE DIGITAL PRESENCE DILEMMA:

In the digital age, an impactful online presence is vital. However, crafting unique, engaging content for various platforms is no small feat. Each social media platform has its own culture and content preferences. Repurposing content across platforms without losing the essence of your message requires creativity and a deep understanding of each platform's algorithm and user behavior. Juggling these demands, along with other business responsibilities, can be overwhelming, often leading to generic or inconsistent online engagement.

ChatGPT revolutionizes this process. It helps to create tailored content for each platform, ensuring that your brand's message resonates with diverse online communities. ChatGPT's ability to adapt content quickly for different formats, such as transforming a blog post into a series of engaging tweets, not only saves time but also enhances brand visibility and engagement, amplifying your digital footprint.

3. FOSTERING CLIENT RELATIONSHIPS:

Client satisfaction is paramount. Delays in product or service delivery, frequent requests for clarification, and slow response times can erode client trust. In a competitive market, businesspeople cannot afford to be seen as unreliable or inefficient. Maintaining high-quality output while managing timely deliveries and clear communication is a juggling act that many struggle with.

ChatGPT emerges as an invaluable partner in this arena. It streamlines and improves communication by generating clear, professional responses and updates for clients and other business stakeholders. It helps create project outlines, proposals, and even detailed reports, significantly reducing turnaround times. With ChatGPT, you can consistently deliver high-quality products and services at a pace that keeps clients satisfied and loyal, solidifying your reputation as a reliable business.

4. UNVEILING NEW REVENUE AVENUES:

Diversifying income streams is a key growth strategy for any business or entrepreneur. However, the exploration of new ventures, like starting a blog, developing a product, or revamping a website, can be daunting. These projects often require a significant investment of time, resources, and specific skills, which might not always be readily available. This barrier can stifle innovation and limit income potential.

ChatGPT acts as a catalyst for business growth by easing the burden of creating and managing new projects. It can generate rich, engaging content for blogs or social media, helping you establish a strong online presence and attract a wider audience. If you're considering launching a new product or service, ChatGPT can help brainstorm ideas, create product descriptions, and even draft marketing strategies. This versatility of ChatGPT means you can explore and execute new ideas with less time and resource investment, paving the way for diversified income streams and business expansion.

5. MASTERING THE ART OF PRICING:

Pricing strategy is critical for business success. Set the price too high, and you risk alienating potential customers; too low, and you might undercut your profits or undervalue your offering. Finding the sweet spot requires a nuanced understanding of consumer behavior, pricing psychology, competitor pricing, and your cost structures. Navigating this complex landscape can be daunting, especially for new entrepreneurs or small businesses with limited market research capabilities.

Leveraging its vast database of market research, consumer trends, and industry analysis, ChatGPT can offer insightful recommendations on pricing strategies. It helps you analyze various factors, from demographic preferences to competitor pricing, enabling you to make data-driven decisions. ChatGPT's insights can guide you in tweaking your pricing models to balance profitability with customer appeal, optimizing your revenue potential.

6. HARNESSING INNOVATIVE TOOLS AND TECHNOLOGIES:

The rapid evolution of technology presents both opportunities and challenges. While new tools can streamline operations and enhance productivity, keeping up with the latest developments and determining their applicability to your specific needs is a time-consuming and often confusing task. The risk of investing in the wrong technology can lead to wasted resources and missed opportunities.

ChatGPT simplifies this process by providing curated recommendations on the latest tools and technologies relevant to your industry and specific business needs. It can suggest software for automation, project management, customer relationship management, and more, tailored to enhance your operational efficiency. By guiding you through the analysis of these tools, ChatGPT helps you stay ahead of the curve, ensuring that your business remains competitive and efficient.

A BROAD SPECTRUM OF CHALLENGES AND OPPORTUNITIES:

Professionals and entrepreneurs, irrespective of their field, grapple with a diverse array of challenges and opportunities. These range from the strategic - like navigating market shifts, to the operational - such as streamlining internal processes. There are also creative challenges, like ideating novel marketing campaigns or designing new products and many more challenges and opportunities.

Each of these challenges, though distinct, shares a common thread—the need for innovative, efficient, and effective solutions. This is where ChatGPT emerges as a versatile partner, equipped to address a broad spectrum of your business needs.

CHARTING YOUR NEXT CHAPTER TO UNLEASH POSSIBILITIES WITH CHATGPT:

As you turn these pages, pause for a moment, and reflect on your own professional or business journey. Think about the hurdles that stand in your way, the dreams that seem just out of reach, and the daily tasks that consume your valuable time.

What are the barriers that hinder your path to achieving more, living more fully, or reaching those ambitious goals? This moment of introspection is an invitation to imagine the transformative impact ChatGPT can have in your life. Envision a tool that not only streamlines your workflow but also fuels your creativity, sharpens your strategies, and elevates your aspirations. ChatGPT is more than just a technological advancement; it's a gateway to redefining what's possible for you.

Begin your exploration into how ChatGPT can be tailored to unlock new potential, solve complex problems, and guide you towards a more fulfilled and successful life. With ChatGPT by your side, the hurdles of the world transform into steppingstones for success. Whatever is the challenge or opportunity you face, ChatGPT is your versatile, intelligent partner. Embrace the power of this revolutionary tool and unlock your full potential.

Let's dive deeper into the key applications of ChatGPT in the following chapters, where we explore key areas, providing you with actionable insights and strategies for success.

<u>Chapter 6</u>
GETTING STARTED WITH CHATGPT

STEP 1: Sign up for an OpenAl account

Go to chat.openai.com and sign up for an OpenAl account. This will provide you with access to ChatGPT.

To get started with an account, just navigate to the OpenAI website and select the 'Sign Up' option. During the registration process, you'll be asked to enter basic details like your name and email address, or sign up with your Google, Microsoft or Apple account, and to accept the terms of service. After you've finished these steps, you'll have your new account ready, and you can log in to explore.

STEP 2: Select Your GPT Model (For Paid Accounts Only)

Upon registering for ChatGPT, there's an option to upgrade to 'ChatGPT Plus' at $20 a month. A key advantage is uninterrupted access to ChatGPT, even when the free version reaches capacity limits.

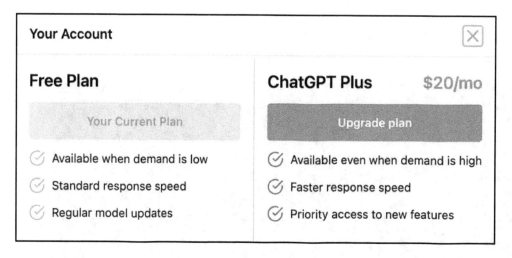

As a ChatGPT Plus user, especially with the introduction of the latest GPT model, you'll find an additional feature: a dropdown menu at the top of the interface, allowing you to select from different models. Opting for the latest GPT model is recommended for optimal results, though we note it comes normally with a limit of 25 messages every three hours. ChatGPT Plus subscription gives you access to GPTs. More on GPTs in a subsequent chapter.

STEP 3: Engage with the ChatGPT Model

After logging in at chat.openai.com, you're ready to interact with the ChatGPT model. Just enter your query in the input field and hit the 'Send' button. ChatGPT will craft a response tailored to your prompt.

Try various prompts and adjust the settings to observe different responses from ChatGPT. You might, for instance, alter the length and tone to gauge their impact on the uniqueness and imaginative quality of the responses. Enter your prompts in the designated area marked

"Message ChatGPT".

STEP 4: ChatGPT in Real-Time Use

Below is an example of ChatGPT in use. You can see a prompt I entered: This is how the ChatGPT interface appears; I encourage you to explore it at chat.openai.com.

I purchased a book about how to use ChatGPT to make money. What recommendations do you have for making the best use of my new book?

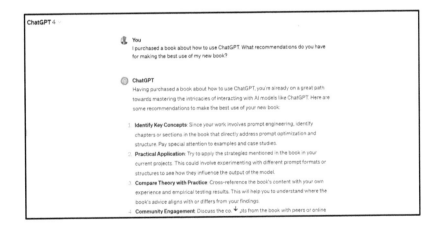

You can start with a basic prompt, probe it with questions, or challenge it with tasks like rewriting their output in a simpler language, translating, analyzing data, summarizing books, suggesting readings, and even brainstorming questions to ask ChatGPT itself.

For optimal utilization of this book, I suggest you employ the prompt that I previously showed and adapt it to your circumstances. This approach will ensure you derive maximum benefit from the contents of the book.

Following with the previous example, I subsequently sent the following prompt to enhance my understanding of ChatGPT response:

> *Please rewrite your output in a more simple language*

And here is ChatGPT new output:

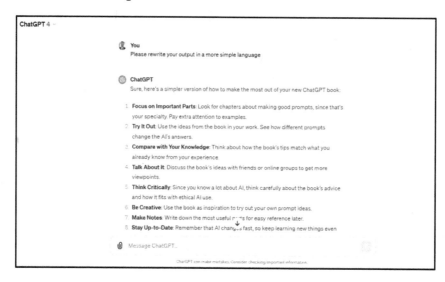

You can basically ask ChatGPT whatever you would like to know or learn. You literally have the entire world's knowledge at our fingertips.

Chapter 7
WHAT ARE PROMPTS?

Prompts are suggestions, questions, or ideas for what and how Chatbots should respond. And for Chatbots to provide helpful responses, Chatbots need a thorough prompt with some background information and relevant data. Becoming a solid prompt writer takes time and experience, but there are also some best practices that you can use to see success quickly:

1. **Be precise in your instructions:** When using ChatGPT for generating income, precision in instructions is crucial. Define your goals, tone, and scope clearly. For example, instruct ChatGPT to "*Create a persuasive sales pitch under 200 words, highlighting our new product's cost-effectiveness for Q1 targets.*
2. **Integrate contextual information:** Incorporate relevant context to enhance ChatGPT response accuracy. Include essential details about your business or market trends when crafting marketing strategies or customer outreach messages.
3. **Segment your interactions:** Divide complex tasks into simpler components. For example, if creating a comprehensive business proposal, use separate prompts for each section - introduction, problem statement, solution, and conclusion.
4. **Continuous refinement:** Use ChatGPT outputs as a foundation, then refine and personalize them to align with your business's unique voice and objectives. This ensures content relevance to your specific financial goals.

5. **Employ follow-up prompts:** For deeper insights, employ follow-up prompts based on initial responses. Start with *"Draft a list of unique selling points for our service"*. And after you receive the response from ChatGPT, you can then follow with *"Develop a detailed explanation for each point, focusing on customer benefits."* This approach enriches the content and makes it more applicable to your business context.

For more detailed best practices, refer to the subsequent Chapter No 9 "FOUNDATIONAL PRINCIPLES FOR USING CHATGPT/GPTs" and Chapter No 10 "BEST PRACTICES TO MASTER CHATGPT PROMPTS".

Chapter 8
HOW TO USE THIS BOOK?

In today's dynamic market, leveraging AI technology like ChatGPT is key to unlocking additional revenue streams and enhancing business efficiency. This book offers a guide to using ChatGPT for financial growth. The book is designed for flexible reading. Jump into sections that align with your immediate business needs. Here are some important considerations for using this book:

- **Prompt Engineering for Effective Strategies:** This book encourages a strategic approach to crafting prompts. All prompts in this book need to be tailored to your specific business objectives and enhanced with the provided best practices to maximize their results. When prompt formulas are shown, terms enclosed in square brackets [ ] are conducive to customization. Again, customize all your prompts to fit your business goals and strategies, experience, or skills for more precise and actionable outputs from ChatGPT.
- **Multi-Faceted Techniques for Tailored Prompts:** Combine best practices for prompting to create unique prompts that meet your specific goals. The effectiveness of your prompts directly influences the quality of ChatGPT responses, making it crucial to invest time in prompt customization.
- **Ethical and Judicious Use of AI:** While ChatGPT offers insightful business advice, it's essential to use it as a starting point, enhancing the suggestions through your expertise and judgment. AI should augment, not replace, human decision-making.
- **Best Practices in Communication:** Maintain a clear and conversational tone with ChatGPT. Open-ended questions elicit more detailed and helpful responses. Setting a specific persona for ChatGPT can also provide tailored advice from a unique business perspective.
- **Defining Audience and Context:** Clearly articulate the target market or sector when using ChatGPT. Whether for business strategies, specific product lines, or market analysis, a well-defined context ensures more relevant and effective prompts.
- **Specialized GPT for Business Growth:** Chapter No 12 "SPECIALIZED GPTs FOR MAXIMIZING EARNINGS" introduces tailored Generative Pre-trained Transformers (GPTs) designed to support specific business goals. These specialized GPTs function as virtual consultants, offering insights and strategies for various aspects of business development. When you interact with ChatGPT, you can direct your prompts to a specific GPT that aligns with your task and topic. This targeted approach ensures that the responses you receive are as customized and relevant as possible, enhancing the precision and effectiveness of the AI's help in your business ventures.
- **Leverage your learning with FREE Bonuses:** Dive into Appendix No 1, 2, and 3 to

unlock exclusive insights and tools. From *'The Simple Guide to Wealth"* in Appendix 1, to 'Over 500 Customizable Prompts' in Appendix 2, and '1100 Follow-up Prompts' in Appendix 3, these resources are your key to enriching interactions with ChatGPT and advancing your journey towards financial independence and mastery over AI conversations.

Chapter 9
FOUNDATIONAL PRINCIPLES FOR USING CHATGPT/GPTs

Using ChatGPT to its fullest capacity requires a strategic approach to human-AI interaction. Consider the process as guiding a highly capable, albeit novice, team member. This perspective helps demystify the intricacies of engaging with sophisticated AI models, such as ChatGPT. To optimize its capabilities, it is necessary to design each interaction, or 'prompt', adhering to these fundamental principles.

1. **CONTEXTUALIZATION:** The cornerstone of effective AI interaction is context. By providing a comprehensive background, you empower ChatGPT to tailor its insights, ensuring alignment with the objectives of your task. Here is an example of a prompt:

   > *Craft a comprehensive guide tailored for small business owners, focusing on the nuances of email-based customer service. Emphasize etiquette and the pivotal role of timely responses, aiming for a narrative that is both informative and engaging, spanning approximately 600 words.*

2. **SEQUENTIAL CLARITY:** Imagine delineating tasks as you would in a meticulously organized checklist. This approach demystifies the process, guiding ChatGPT through a logical progression of steps, enhancing the accuracy and relevance of its outputs. Here is an example of a prompt:

   > *Distill the essence of this 30-minute sales discourse into a concise summary not exceeding 300 words. Highlight the core issues addressed, the proposed solutions, their benefits, and actionable next steps, ensuring a coherent and accessible narrative.*

3. **EXEMPLIFICATION:** Providing examples helps to set benchmarks for the expected deliverables. It offers ChatGPT a concrete model to emulate, ensuring that the outcomes resonate with your predefined standards. Here is an example of a prompt:

   > *Produce a job profile for a Senior Analyst, delineating responsibilities, expected deliverables, and requisite competencies, with an emphasis on forward-thinking skills pertinent to 2024. Draw inspiration from the structure, tone, and complexity of a previously used job description for a similar role, which is provided herein: [insert example]*

In the following chapter, we will explore a comprehensive range of best practices aimed at enhancing your proficiency in crafting prompts. This endeavor maximizes the benefits derived from this revolutionary AI tool, integrating advanced methodologies and strategic insights in prompt engineering.

Chapter 10
BEST PRACTICES TO MASTER PROMPTS

Consider this: you're about to launch a new product or tackle a new business project, but you're unsure where to start. This is where ChatGPT prompts come in, serving as your digital compass to navigate the world of AI-assisted tasks. Prompts are the critical inputs you give to ChatGPT. They aren't just random questions or statements; they are strategic tools designed to elicit the most effective, relevant, and precise responses from ChatGPT.

Whether you're a professional seeking to enhance your business strategies, an entrepreneur exploring new ventures, or an individual launching a side-hustle, mastering the art of prompt crafting is essential. Here are some key best practices:

1. IMPLEMENTING PRECISION IN INSTRUCTIONS:

In the realm of conversational AI, the precision of your instructions plays a crucial role in determining the effectiveness and relevance of the responses you receive. This principle is especially crucial when dealing with complex tasks like developing a content strategy for a niche blog, where every detail can significantly impact the results.

For example, let's imagine you're working on a content strategy for a health and wellness blog.

Less effective ✕ :

Create blog topics for a wellness blog.

This prompt lacks specificity regarding the blog's target audience, the type of wellness content (physical, mental, spiritual), and the blog's unique angle or approach.

Better ☑ :

Generate 5 unique blog topics focused on holistic mental wellness for young professionals, emphasizing mindfulness techniques and work-life balance.

This prompt clearly defines the blog's niche (holistic mental wellness), target audience (young professionals), and specific content areas (mindfulness techniques, work-life balance), enabling ChatGPT to produce more targeted and relevant blog topic suggestions.

Through precise instructions, you can guide ChatGPT to generate outputs that are not only relevant and tailored to your specific needs, but also aligned with your objectives.

2. EMPHASIZING CONTEXT AS KING:

The context you provide is paramount to getting accurate and valuable outputs. Context guides the AI to better understand the nuances of your query and to deliver more customized responses. This is especially relevant in fields like marketing, where the specifics of a product, its target audience, and brand values can significantly influence the strategy.

Consider a scenario where you're planning a marketing strategy for a niche product, such as an eco-friendly clothing line targeted at college students.

Less effective ✕:

> *I need promotional strategies for a clothing line.*

This prompt is vague and lacks the crucial details that define the product and its audience. It doesn't mention the eco-friendly nature of the clothing line, the target demographic of college students, the use of recycled materials, or the alignment with sustainability causes.

Better ☑:

> *I'm launching a budget-friendly marketing campaign for 'GreenThreads', a new eco-friendly clothing line designed for college students. Our unique selling point is the use of recycled materials and active support for global sustainability causes. Can you suggest innovative promotional strategies that resonate with these values and engage a young, environmentally conscious audience?*

This prompt effectively sets the scene, detailing the product ('GreenThreads', an eco-friendly clothing line), the target demographic (college students) and unique features (recycled materials, support for sustainability).

With the appropriate context, ChatGPT response is going to be specific and align with your needs. This can result in strategies that are on-target, relevant, and effective for the intended audience and brand values.

3. BREAKING DOWN THE TASK:

One of the most effective strategies in prompt engineering is to break down larger, more complex tasks into smaller, more manageable components. This approach, known as task segmentation, is useful when dealing with intricate projects that involve multiple elements.

For complex tasks like event planning, breaking down the overall task into smaller, focused prompts can help manage each aspect more efficiently. The separate prompts for planning a personal event can be:

Venue Selection:

> *List three suitable venues in downtown Chicago for a 30-person birthday party, focusing on outdoor options with catering facilities.*

Guest List Creation:

> *Draft an invitation list for the birthday party, considering close family members and friends, totaling up to 30 people.*

Menu Planning:

> *Suggest a catering menu for the party that includes vegetarian, vegan, and gluten-free options.*

By dividing the task into discrete, focused prompts, you can guide ChatGPT to address each aspect of the project individually, ensuring thoroughness and attention to detail.

4. SPECIFICALLY CONTEXTUALIZING RESPONSES:

Specific contextualization involves providing detailed background information that sets the stage for the AI's response. This practice helps the AI to tailor its responses to fit the precise scenario you're dealing with, leading to more accurate and relevant results.

Less effective ✕ :

> *Tell me about investing in energy.*

This prompt lacks specificity and context, making it too broad and ambiguous. Without details on the type of energy investment, geographical focus, or the financial scope, ChatGPT might produce generic content that addresses no practical investment strategies or market trends, resulting in less valuable information for the reader.

Better ☑ :

> *Given the current market trends in renewable energy, analyze the long-term financial benefits of investing in solar panels for residential properties in Arizona.*

This prompt is correctly contextualized as it focuses on a specific market (renewable energy), a particular financial aspect (long-term benefits), a type of investment (solar panels), and a defined location (residential properties in Arizona). This level of detail helps ChatGPT understand the precise nature of the inquiry, leading to more targeted and relevant content.

It emphasizes the importance of providing ChatGPT with clear and detailed information to generate useful content for those looking to make informed decisions, particularly in complex fields such as investment and market analysis.

5. CONDUCTING COMPARATIVE ANALYSIS:

Comparative analysis prompts ask the AI to weigh distinct elements against each other. This is a strategic way of prompting that encourages the AI to consider the pros and cons of each item, providing a balanced view that can be instrumental in decision-making processes.

Less effective ✕ :

> *Which is better for marketing, Instagram or TikTok?*

This prompt is too vague and lacks criteria for "better," making it challenging for ChatGPT to provide a meaningful comparison. It doesn't specify the metrics, target audience, or goals of the marketing campaign, leading to a potentially superficial analysis that might not serve the reader's strategic needs.

Better ☑️ :

> *Compare the user engagement metrics of Instagram Reels and TikTok videos for digital marketing campaigns targeting Gen Z in the United States.*

This prompt correctly asks for a comparative analysis between two similar yet distinct platforms, focusing on a specific metric (user engagement), a target audience (Gen Z), and a geographical region (the United States). It enables ChatGPT to create a focused comparison relevant to digital marketers interested in optimizing their strategies for a young American audience.

6. REFINING AND PERSONALIZING OUTPUTS:

Outputs from ChatGPT are a starting point. Customize its responses to fit your personal or business needs and wants. This ensures the result truly reflects your goals and style. After generating an initial draft, refining, and personalizing the content can ensure it aligns with your unique style or brand. Your prompt then can be:

> *Based on the draft marketing plan for our handmade jewelry business, please revise the social media section to reflect a more personal, story-driven approach, highlighting the artisanal process and the cultural heritage behind our products.*

This follow-up prompt not only tailors the content to be more brand specific but also adds depth and authenticity, making it more appealing to the target audience. ChatGPT can provide a solid foundation or draft, but the magic lies in your ability to mold that content to resonate with your specific goals, brand ethos, or personal touch.

7. USING FOLLOW-UP PROMPTS:

Utilizing follow-up prompts in your interactions with ChatGPT is a powerful technique to deepen the exploration of a subject or to elaborate on an initial idea. It allows you to refine the AI's outputs, progressively transforming a broad concept into a well-defined plan or a fleshed-out idea.

To delve deeper into a topic or idea, using follow-up prompts can help explore and expand on the initial output. For example, start with the prompt:

> *Generate a list of innovative product ideas for home office workers.*

And you can then submit this follow-up prompt:

> *For the idea from the list that has the highest probability of success, provide a detailed*

This best practice is especially effective in iterative brainstorming sessions or when developing complex projects that require multiple stages of planning and refinement. Appendix No 3 offers 1100 generic follow-up prompts. Remember, the key is to adapt these follow-up prompts to your specific context, whether you're steering a business project, embarking on a personal endeavor, or simply exploring the vast capabilities of ChatGPT.

8. CRAFTING PRECISE PROMPTS:

In the realm of prompt engineering with ChatGPT, precision is paramount. Your prompts should encapsulate every necessary element to construct a response that aligns perfectly with your needs. The key to harnessing the full potential of ChatGPT lies in the specificity of your prompts.

Be descriptive and detailed about the desired context, outcome, length, format, style, and any other relevant aspects. This approach is akin to providing ChatGPT with a finely tuned set of instructions, enabling it to generate responses that are not only relevant but also tailored to your precise requirements.

Less effective ✕:

Write a poem about OpenAI.

This prompt, while clear, lacks the specificity needed to guide ChatGPT towards creating a piece that resonates with your specific intent or audience. The result might be good, but it might not align with your vision.

Better ☑:

Write a short, inspiring poem about OpenAI, focusing on the recent DALL-E product launch.

This prompt is clear, guiding ChatGPT to not only craft a poem about OpenAI but to do so in a way that highlights a specific aspect—the DALL-E product launch—in an inspiring tone.

9. STRUCTURING PROMPTS FOR ENHANCED CLARITY:

One important strategy in prompt engineering with ChatGPT involves placing instructions at the beginning of the prompt and using specific symbols like ### or triple quotes """" to separate the instruction from the context.

This technique not only adds clarity but also helps in delineating the boundaries of the request, ensuring that ChatGPT accurately understands and executes the task. A well-structured prompt leads to more accurate and useful responses.

Less effective ✕:

> *Summarize the text below as a bullet point list of the most important points.*
>
> *[Insert text input here]*

In this less effective example, the prompt blends into the text input, which can lead to confusion or misinterpretation.

Better ☑ **:**

> *Summarize the text below as a bullet point list of the most important points.*
>
> *Text:*
>
> *###[Insert text input here]###*

Note that *[Insert text input here]* is a placeholder for actual text.

In this improved example, the clear separation using triple ### distinctly outlines the text input. Including 'Text:' further clarifies the prompt, making it clear to ChatGPT that what follows is the material to be summarized. This structure is useful for more complex tasks where multiple elements or types of input are involved.

By adopting this structured approach in crafting your prompts, you can enhance the efficiency and effectiveness of your interactions with ChatGPT. This method can be beneficial when dealing with lengthy or complex texts, where clarity in instructions and a well-defined structure are crucial for obtaining the desired outcome.

10. FOCUSING ON SPECIFICITY AND CLARITY IN PROMPTS:

Mastering the art of effective communication with ChatGPT is crucial for obtaining the exact responses you need. For example, imagine you're brainstorming ideas for a side hustle to generate extra income. To harness ChatGPT's potential in this context, a well-constructed prompt is key. You can use this prompt:

> *Provide five unique side hustle ideas that can be started with minimal investment and have the potential for high returns.*

By being clear and specific in your request, ChatGPT can offer tailored, creative solutions that align with your goals, helping you embark on a rewarding entrepreneurial journey.

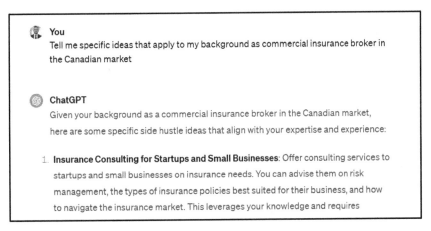

You
Provide five unique side hustle ideas that can be started with minimal investment and have the potential for high returns.

ChatGPT
Certainly! Here are five unique side hustle ideas that require minimal investment but hold the potential for high returns:

1. **Social Media Management for Small Businesses**: Many small businesses struggle to maintain an active social media presence. With your knowledge of social media trends and basic marketing, you can offer to manage their social media accounts, create content, and engage with their audience. This requires minimal investment, mostly your time and a good internet connection.
2. **Online Tutoring or Coaching**: If you have expertise in a particular subject, language, or skill, you can start an online tutoring or coaching service. This can be done through

Upon receiving a generic response from ChatGPT, you might realize that the suggestions don't precisely fit your unique circumstances, available resources, or skill set. To refine the output and make it more applicable to your situation, a follow-up prompt becomes essential.

You can enhance your prompt with additional specifics, such as the following prompt:

Tell me specific ideas that apply to my background as a commercial insurance broker in the Canadian market.

Here is ChatGPT's output:

You
Tell me specific ideas that apply to my background as commercial insurance broker in the Canadian market

ChatGPT
Given your background as a commercial insurance broker in the Canadian market, here are some specific side hustle ideas that align with your expertise and experience:

1. **Insurance Consulting for Startups and Small Businesses**: Offer consulting services to startups and small businesses on insurance needs. You can advise them on risk management, the types of insurance policies best suited for their business, and how to navigate the insurance market. This leverages your knowledge and requires

After receiving a varied list of suggestions, you might find that certain ideas, like offering consulting services, don't align with your preferences. If your aim is to harness the potential of the internet and social media, for example, further specificity in your follow-up prompt is key.

You could refine your request with a new follow-up prompt:

I appreciate these suggestions, but my focus is on opportunities that can be only pursued through the Internet and social media. Could you provide ideas tailored to this area?

Two key insights emerge from this exercise:

First, the nature of responses from ChatGPT dramatically shifts with each change in the prompt. Each time I clarified my preferences, ChatGPT recalibrated its suggestions, demonstrating an understanding beyond mere keyword matching. For instance, indicating my preference for internet and social media redirected the entire set of recommendations, not just tweaking individual aspects. Similarly, if I had expressed a liking for another subject, the responses would have uniquely catered to those interests.

Second, the process didn't require reiterating the entire context with each follow-up. ChatGPT efficiently kept the original conversation thread - in this case, the quest for side-hustle ideas. This ability to understand and build upon previous interactions with no need to repeat context makes ChatGPT an exceptionally powerful tool in tailoring responses to specific and evolving requests.

11. CREATING CREATIVE SCENARIOS:

This technique involves crafting prompts that encourage imaginative thinking and creative output. This technique is useful when you want to explore innovative ideas or speculative scenarios that might not yet exist.

Less effective ✕:

> *Tell me about future communication methods.*

The less effective prompt misses the chance to engage the AI's creative capabilities by presenting a generic request about future communication. Lacking detail, the prompt risks eliciting a response that overlooks nuanced considerations and innovative aspects.

Better ☑:

> *Imagine a future where telepathic communication is the norm. Describe the impact this would have on personal privacy and public interactions in urban settings.*

This example invites ChatGPT to imagine an advanced form of communication, setting the stage for an in-depth analysis of its societal implications. It specifically asks to consider the effects on privacy and public life, steering the AI to produce focused and insightful content that predicts future societal dynamics.

With this technique, you can add the following phrases to your prompts to get insightful, innovative responses:

- *"Identify latent opportunities and avant-garde approaches."*
- *"Unveil under-the-radar tactics and groundbreaking schemes."*
- *"Spotlight inventive ideas and future-forward answers."*
- *"Elaborate on fresh perspectives and audacious strategies."*
- *"Delve into uncharted territories and groundbreaking concepts."*
- *"Investigate unexpected avenues and creative pathways."*
- *"Suggest fresh approaches and unique strategies."*

12. ENGAGING IN ROLE PLAY AND SIMULATION:

Role play and simulation involve prompting ChatGPT to adopt a specific character or professional persona, which can be a powerful way to generate responses that require empathy, specialized knowledge, or a particular perspective.

Less effective ✕:

> *Talk about climate change over the past 30 years.*

The less effective example's generality results in a missed opportunity for creative storytelling and personalized insight. The lack of a role-play element likely leads to a response that is a straightforward recount of climate change events, without the depth or the personalized touch that the role-playing prompt could have inspired.

Better ☑:

> *You are a climate scientist in the year 2050 looking back at the climate actions taken in the past 30 years. Write a retrospective report on the effectiveness of these actions.*

In the better example, the role of a future climate scientist guides ChatGPT, framing the response within a retrospective and analytical perspective. It's a prompt that elicits a nuanced narrative, reflecting on decades of climate action, thus expected to yield a response filled with introspection and detailed examination.

13. ENHANCING OUTPUT PRECISION WITH EXAMPLES:

When interacting with ChatGPT, one key effective way to guide the AI towards your desired output is to articulate the format requirements through examples. By doing so, you provide a concrete template for ChatGPT to follow, ensuring that the response aligns closely with your expectations.

Less effective ✕:

> *Extract the entities mentioned in the text below. Extract the following 4 entity types: company names, people names, specific topics and themes.*
>
> *Text: [Insert text here]*

In this example, while the task is clear, the lack of a specified format can lead to varied interpretations and outputs. The response might be accurate in content but may not align with your specific requirements for data organization or presentation.

Better ☑:

> *Extract the entities mentioned in the text below. First extract all company names, then extract all people's names, then extract specific topics which fit the content and finally extract general overarching themes.*
>
> *Desired format:*
> *Company names: [Company Name 1], [Company Name 2], [Company Name 3]*
> *People's names: [Name 1], [Name 2], [Name 3]*
> *Specific topics: [Topic 1], [Topic 2], [Topic 3]*
> *General themes: [Theme 1], [Theme 2], [Theme 3]*
>
> *Separate the company names, people's names, specific topics and general themes with commas.*
>
> *Text: "[Insert text here]"*

This enhanced prompt does more than just specify the task; it also illustrates the exact format in which you want the information presented. This level of detail in the prompt, particularly the inclusion of a template for the output, can significantly improve the relevance and usability of the ChatGPT response.

This structured approach is especially useful when dealing with data extraction or categorization tasks. By outlining the format in a clear manner, you make it easier to parse multiple outputs.

14. STREAMLINING DESCRIPTIONS FOR PRECISION AND CLARITY:

An essential aspect of effective prompting is the elimination of vague, 'fluffy' descriptions in favor of concise and precise instructions. The clarity of your prompts directly influences the quality and relevance of ChatGPT responses. By reducing ambiguity and providing exact specifications, you guide ChatGPT to generate content that aligns perfectly with your requirements.

Less effective ✕:

> *The description for this product should be fairly short, a few sentences only and not too much more.*

In this less effective prompt, the instructions are vague. Terms like "fairly short" and "not too much more" are open to interpretation, which can lead to a wide range of outputs in terms of length and detail.

Better ☑:

> *The description for this product should be 3 to 5-sentences and written in a professional writing format.*

This better prompt exemplifies clarity and specificity. Setting clear boundaries and expectations for the output, you specify that the description should be contained within a 3 to 5 sentence paragraph. This approach is crucial, especially in scenarios where content needs to fit specific criteria and format, such as character limits in advertising copy or conciseness in product descriptions.

15. GUIDING CHATGPT WITH CONSTRUCTIVE INSTRUCTIONS:

Effective communication with ChatGPT involves not only stating what to avoid but also clearly defining what to do instead. This approach transforms your prompts from mere prohibitions to constructive guides that lead to more productive and accurate responses from ChatGPT.

Less effective ✗:

Do not give me a generic response. I need something unique.

This prompt, while indicating what ChatGPT should avoid, failing to provide exact direction on what ChatGPT should do instead.

Better ☑:

Do not give me a generic response. Craft a response that incorporates innovative ideas and unique perspectives, steering clear of common clichés. Aim for originality and creativity.

This enhanced prompt effectively guides ChatGPT on how to handle its output. It not only specifies what ChatGPT should not provide but also clearly outlines what it should provide instead.

16. CLARIFYING ABSTRACT CONCEPTS:

Abstract concept clarification is a prompting technique in ChatGPT where the AI is tasked with explaining or simplifying complex, abstract, or high-level concepts. This approach is vital for making intricate ideas more accessible and understandable to a broader audience. It involves breaking down sophisticated topics into fundamental components and presenting them in a clear, concise manner.

This technique is beneficial in educational contexts, technical discussions, or whenever detailed concepts need to be conveyed to those unfamiliar with the subject.

Less effective ✗:

Explain Blockchain Technology.

This prompt lacks specificity regarding the audience's understanding level and fails to instruct ChatGPT to simplify the concept. The AI might provide a standard, possibly technical explanation, which could be too complex for those without prior knowledge of the topic, leading to confusion rather than clarity.

Better ☑️ **:**

Clarify the concept of 'Blockchain Technology' in simple terms, suitable for someone with no technical background.

This better prompt effectively asks ChatGPT to demystify a complex technological concept. By requesting a simplified explanation suitable for a non-technical audience, the AI is directed to distill the essence of blockchain technology into its most basic and understandable form, making the information accessible to everyone.

17. ENHANCING ACCURACY WITH REFERENCE TEXTS:

In the world of AI and language models like ChatGPT, the phenomenon of inventing responses, particularly for obscure or specialized topics, is not uncommon. To mitigate this and enhance the reliability of the responses, a key tactic is to provide reference texts. Reference texts can guide ChatGPT to respond with information grounded in reality, reducing the tendency to hallucinate answers.

By doing so, you can direct the model to use this information to formulate its responses, thus increasing the factual accuracy of its answers. For example, you could use this prompt:

Use the provided articles delimited by triple quotes to answer my questions. If the answer cannot be found in the articles, write 'I could not find an answer.'

"""insert article 1"""
"""insert article 2"""
"""insert article n"""

[Insert your questions here]

In this approach, the instructions clearly define how ChatGPT should use the provided reference texts. Using triple quotes effectively separates the reference articles from the rest of the text, making it easy for the model to identify and refer to them while formulating a response. This method is akin to providing a researcher with a set of source documents to reference in their study - it guides their analysis and ensures that the conclusions drawn are based on verifiable information.

Instruct ChatGPT to answer with citations from a reference text:

A critical aspect of enhancing the accuracy and reliability of ChatGPT responses, especially in academic or research-oriented contexts, involves instructing the model to include citations from provided reference texts. This approach not only grounds the model's answers in verifiable sources but also allows for the systematic verification of the information through programmatic string matching within the given documents.

When you supplement ChatGPT with relevant, authoritative texts, you can direct it to reference specific passages from these texts in its responses. This method ensures that the answers are not only accurate but also traceable to their sources, significantly enhancing the credibility of the information provided.

For example, you could use this prompt:

> *You will be provided with a document delimited by triple quotes and a question. Your task is to answer the question using only the provided document and to cite the passage(s) of the document used to answer the question. If the document does not contain the information needed to answer this question then simply write: 'Insufficient information'. If an answer to the question is provided, it must be annotated with a citation. Use the following format to cite relevant passages: "{'citation': ...}"*
>
> *"[Insert document here]"*
>
> *My question is: [Insert your question here]*

This structured approach mimics scholarly research practices, where referencing and citations are crucial for validating claims and arguments. By instructing ChatGPT to cite the specific parts of the document it used to formulate an answer, the model effectively functions like a researcher who backs up statements with evidence from the literature.

This tactic enhances the transparency of the AI's thought process. By clearly showing which parts of the provided document influenced its response, ChatGPT offers a window into its reasoning, allowing you to understand how it arrived at a particular conclusion. The clear definition of the format for citations not only aids in understanding the response but also enables easy verification of the cited information.

18. ENGAGING IN PROGRESSIVE INQUIRY:

Progressive inquiry is a method where you can lead ChatGPT through a series of interconnected queries. This technique is especially useful when exploring complex topics that require a multi-faceted or chronological understanding. The key is to start with foundational information and progressively delve deeper, layer by layer, into the subject. This approach not only enriches the depth of the content provided but also ensures that the AI maintains a focused and logical trajectory throughout the conversation.

Less effective ✕:

> *Tell me about AI in cars.*

The less effective example is vague and lacks progression, which may lead to a cursory overview lacking depth. The AI is not prompted to explore the evolution or future implications of AI in the automotive sector, which would likely result in a response that is informative but superficial and not as actionable or insightful.

Better ☑:

> *Considering the exponential growth of AI technology, begin by outlining its early*

This better example effectively uses the progressive inquiry approach, beginning with a historical overview and gradually moving towards current developments and future predictions. The prompt is structured to guide ChatGPT through a logical sequence that builds upon each stage, ensuring a comprehensive exploration of AI's impact on the automotive industry.

19. APPLYING A PROBLEM-SOLVING FRAMEWORK:

The problem-solving framework is all about breaking down complex problems into manageable parts and seeking methodical solutions. When faced with a challenge, this approach guides ChatGPT to dissect the issue systematically and provides step-by-step resolutions.

It's effective for scenarios requiring analytical thinking and strategic planning. The framework encourages ChatGPT to consider various factors and implications, resulting in a comprehensive and practical response that addresses the core of the problem.

Less effective ✕:

How do you fix AI issues in old factory machines?

The less effective prompt is imprecise and open-ended, which could cause a general response lacking specific solutions. Without a clear problem-solving framework or context, the AI might not provide the detailed guidance necessary to address the complex challenge of updating legacy systems with AI technology.

Better ✅:

Diagnose the steps required to mitigate the risks associated with integrating AI into legacy manufacturing systems, considering potential operational disruptions and workforce implications. Let's think about this step by step.

The better prompt clearly defines a problem and asks for a step-by-step solution, considering specific challenges and broader implications. This approach enables ChatGPT to deliver a targeted and structured response, focusing on practical and strategic solutions to integrate AI within established manufacturing processes.

20. LEVERAGING EXAMPLES FOR FEW-SHOT PROMPTING:

In the art of prompt engineering, providing general instructions is typically efficient for guiding ChatGPT responses. However, there are scenarios where explicitly describing a task is challenging, and in such cases, demonstrating through examples becomes invaluable.

This method, known as "few-shot" prompting, involves presenting a series of examples to ChatGPT, which it then uses as a template for its responses. It's effective when you want the model to mimic a specific style or tone that's difficult to articulate in plain instructions. Consider the following example:

Respond in a style that is motivational and uplifting, using metaphors and similes. Give me an inspirational quote about pursuing dreams.

ChatGPT response:

A dream is like a star; it might seem distant, but with persistence, you can reach it.

Consider then this follow-up prompt:

Now, give me an inspirational quote about overcoming challenges.

ChatGPT response:

Overcoming a challenge is like climbing a mountain; the journey may be tough, but the view from the top is breathtaking.

21. SETTING TARGET LENGTH FOR PRECISE OUTPUTS:

In structuring prompts for ChatGPT, one key aspect is the length and format of the output. By specifying the desired length, you can tailor the model's responses to fit specific formats or constraints, such as word counts for an article summary, bullet points for a presentation, or paragraphs for a report.

However, it's important to note that while ChatGPT can approximate the length of its responses, it may not always be exact, especially when asked to generate content with a specific word count. Here is an example of prompt:

Create a summary of the following text in 3 bullet points.

Text: "[Insert text here]"

In this case, you can ask for a bullet-point summary, allowing ChatGPT to focus on extracting and presenting the three most crucial points from the text. The bullet point format naturally lends itself to concise and focused responses, making it an effective way to ensure brevity and relevance in the output. Here is another example:

Summarize the text delimited by triple quotes in about 50 words.

Text: "[Insert text here]"

In this scenario, you can request a summary of a provided text but limit the response to approximately 50 words. This instruction helps ChatGPT focus on condensing the key points of the text into a concise summary. It's important to understand that while ChatGPT aims to meet the word count, the precision of hitting exactly 50 words can vary.

Specifying the desired output length in terms of paragraphs or bullet points tends to yield more reliable results. This is because these formats have more defined structures, making it easier for ChatGPT to adhere to the request.

22. EXPLORING OPPOSING VIEWPOINTS:

Opposing viewpoint exploration in ChatGPT prompting is a technique that involves requesting the AI to consider or debate different perspectives on a topic. This approach is highly beneficial for understanding multifaceted issues, encouraging critical thinking, and uncovering potential biases. By exploring contrasting views, ChatGPT can provide a balanced and comprehensive insight, allowing for a deeper appreciation of complex subjects.

Less effective ✖:

> *Tell me about remote work*

This less effective prompt is too vague and lacks the opposing viewpoints element. ChatGPT response may lean towards a general description of remote work without the depth and balance achieved by contrasting different perspectives.

Better ☑:

> *Assess the impact of remote work on a startup, analyzing its advantages and challenges from the standpoint of both the founding team and the employees. Consider aspects such as work-life balance, collaboration efficiency, cost savings, and potential barriers to communication.*

This prompt effectively engages ChatGPT in contrasting viewpoint analysis by specifying two different perspectives on the same issue. It leads to a nuanced discussion that considers the topic from multiple angles, offering a well-rounded understanding.

23. REQUESTING TEMPORAL SEQUENCE:

Temporal sequence request involves structuring prompts to guide ChatGPT through a chronological analysis or storytelling. This technique is useful for topics where the order of events or phases is crucial, such as historical events, project planning, or life cycle analysis. It helps in receiving structured and coherent responses that respect the natural progression of time.

Less effective ✖:

> *Tell me about a startup's growth.*

Lacking a temporal sequence, this prompt might lead to a disjointed or general overview of a startup's growth. The response may miss the chronological clarity and detailed progression that the correct usage would elicit.

Better ✅ :

> *Outline in a chronological order the major phases of a startup's growth from inception to IPO, highlighting key milestones in each phase.*

This prompt correctly employs the temporal sequence request by asking ChatGPT to follow a startup's journey chronologically. The AI is guided to structure the response in a logical sequence, providing clarity and a comprehensive view of the startup lifecycle.

24. ALLOWING CHATGPT SPACE TO 'THINK':

In the landscape of AI, the concept of "thinking" is metaphorical, yet it serves an essential function when engaging with models like ChatGPT. Just as humans need moments to reflect and consider their responses, ChatGPT benefits from structured prompts that allow it to "reason" through a problem or question.

Patience in Prompt Engineering:

Giving the model time to 'think' is a strategy that allows you to pose your prompts in a way that ChatGPT processes the input thoroughly before delivering an output. This can involve breaking down complex tasks into simpler steps, using a chain of reasoning, or structuring the prompt to facilitate a more thoughtful response.

Instruct the Model to Work it out Slowly:

Instead of expecting instant responses, especially for complex queries, structure your prompts to encourage the model to consider each part of the problem before providing an answer. For example, instead of directly asking for the solution, guide the model through the reasoning steps one by one. Here are a couple of examples of prompts:

> *Let's think about this step by step. The question is: How do we determine the target market for our new product? First, could you guide me through the process of identifying key characteristics of our potential customers?*

> *I'm aiming to streamline our company's financial planning. Could you detail the initial step in devising a monthly budget for our business operations, and then let's explore each following step sequentially?*

You can insert the following phrases into your prompts:

- *"Let's sequentially address each element."*
- *"Let's tackle this in a phased manner."*
- *"Let's think about this step by step."*
- *"Let's go through this systematically."*
- *"Let's dissect this carefully."*
- *"Let's consider each facet of this topic."*

Use Inner Monologue or Sequential Queries:

Implementing an inner monologue technique in your prompts can mimic the human process of thinking out loud, providing ChatGPT with a framework to present its reasoning process. Similarly, sequential queries, where each question builds on the last, can lead ChatGPT through a logical progression of thought. Here are a couple of examples of prompts:

> *Envision you're an entrepreneur analyzing a market opportunity. Guide me through your thought process in identifying the key factors contributing to the opportunity, beginning with market research to understand the demand, and then engaging with potential customers to validate your business idea.*

> *Let's explore the process of product development. Begin by detailing what happens when a customer need is identified, and then describe each subsequent step as if you're an entrepreneur unraveling the path from concept to market-ready product, considering customer feedback, prototype development, and iteration.*

Ask the Model if it Missed Anything on Previous Passes:

After receiving an initial response, follow up with a prompt that asks ChatGPT to review its previous reasoning and check if any steps were overlooked. This iterative approach not only refines the answer but also enhances the model's accuracy and reliability. Here are a couple of examples of prompts:

> *Following your overview of the product launch cycle, could you revisit the explanation and inform me if any crucial detail or phase in the process might require additional elaboration or if you inadvertently overlooked anything?*

> *Reflecting on our analysis of common pitfalls in startup failures, could we revisit the aspects discussed? Is there a particular reason or factor that warrants deeper examination or that we haven't fully addressed yet?*

25. PREDICTING FUTURE SCENARIOS:

Future prediction in ChatGPT prompting involves asking the AI to forecast or speculate about potential future scenarios based on current trends, data, or patterns. This approach is beneficial for strategic planning, trend analysis, and preparing for possible outcomes. It encourages ChatGPT to use its training data to make educated guesses about the future.

Less effective ✕:

> *Tell me about potential opportunities to generate extra income.*

This prompt lacks a future-focused perspective and will probably result in a general overview of opportunities to generate money, missing the opportunity to explore future trends and circumstances.

Better ✓:

Considering the current advancements in technology, like ChatGPT, what are the potential opportunities to generate extra income we might see in the next 1 to 3 years?

This prompt effectively directs ChatGPT to use its knowledge base to speculate on future opportunities to make money, providing a forward-looking perspective based on current developments.

26. PROVIDING META-INSTRUCTIVE PROMPTS:

The meta-instructive prompt technique involves asking ChatGPT to generate a prompt itself, essentially creating a 'prompt for a prompt.' This approach is useful when you want to explore how ChatGPT would structure a query or task for itself or another AI, based on given criteria or objectives. It encourages creative and self-reflective AI usage, where the AI not only responds to prompts but also conceptualizes them.

Less effective ✕ :

Write a sample chapter for a self-help book.

This prompt directly asks for a sample chapter, which is straightforward but doesn't use ChatGPT's ability to conceptualize broader ghostwriting opportunities.

Better ☑ :

Create a prompt that would challenge you, as ChatGPT, to outline innovative and marketable themes for a ghostwritten self-help book.

This meta-instructive prompt motivates ChatGPT to come up by itself with a prompt, which you can subsequently submit to ChatGPT to get various engaging and potentially profitable themes for a self-help book. In this example, this can be valuable for ghostwriters seeking unique angles in a competitive market. This approach not only generates content but also helps in identifying market trends and niches in the ghostwriting domain.

27. EXPLORING VARIOUS POSSIBILITIES:

Test different prompts and settings. For example, you can submit to ChatGPT the following prompt:

Craft an inspiring message that motivates me to kick start my side-hustle idea, infused with an uplifting writing style.

Or, for a more personalized touch, guide ChatGPT to emulate the style of renowned figures. See the following prompt:

Compose an encouraging message in the tone of voice of Tony Robbins to propel me into action on my side-hustle concept.

Each unique prompt can lead to the discovery of new and effective ways to generate content that resonates with you and your goals. Embrace the art of experimentation with ChatGPT. Venturing into various prompts and settings can unlock creative avenues you might not have previously considered. For generating content, the possibilities are boundless.

28. USING THE 'ACT AS' APPROACH:

Unlocking personalized, high-value content from ChatGPT is a breeze with this ingenious approach. By using the directive of "Act as a...", you can explore its potential with the following example:

Act as a business coach specializing in entrepreneurial growth. Devise innovative strategies for augmenting subscriber numbers for my newsletter business. Explore various themes as money management, personal finance, or other engaging topics. The goal is to select a theme that resonates profoundly with my target audience, primarily professionals.

Chapter 18 "ACT AS PROMPTS FOR DIVERSE PROFESSIONS" has a list of the right professionals for launching your business.

29. ACCESSING TAILORED RESPONSES FROM CHATGPT:

Should ChatGPT's initial reply fall short of expectations, refining its output is within your reach. You can guide the model towards a more precise answer with prompts such as

Revise your previous response to align more closely with [Insert your requirements].

Or

Adjust your previous answer to incorporate my specific criteria regarding [Insert your criteria].

Alternatively, you can request:

Please rephrase the last response to enhance its clarity and detail.

This approach prompts ChatGPT to rework its original answer, providing you with revised or varied responses that might better align with your needs.

30. OPTIMIZING CHOICES THROUGH MULTIPLE RESPONSES:

When seeking the ideal option for elements like email subjects or blog titles, having a range of choices can be instrumental. This approach is beneficial for crafting attention-grabbing email subjects to approach prospects or for generating compelling titles for your entrepreneurship blog.

It's common not to find the perfect choice at the first attempt, so leveraging ChatGPT to provide multiple suggestions at once can be a game-changer. For instance, you can send the following prompts:

Act as a marketing expert, provide 5 intriguing subject lines for reaching out to young adults about life insurance plans

Or

Craft ten captivating titles for a blog post discussing innovative digital wall art ventures on Etsy.com.

These prompts will yield a variety of options, allowing you to select the most fitting one.

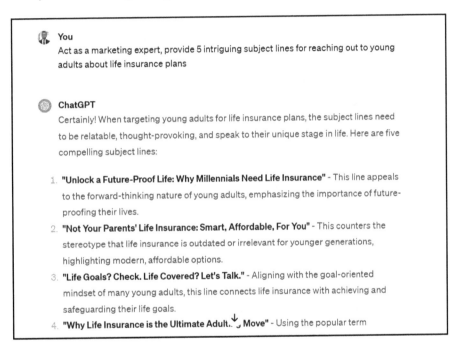

31. ENHANCING CONTENT WITH PRECISION:

While ChatGPT is a remarkable resource for crafting high-quality content, it's essential to remember that it serves as an initial draft rather than a final product. A crucial step in the process involves human intervention to refine and polish the output.

Carefully reviewing and editing the generated text is vital to eliminate errors and tailor it to your specific requirements. This practice ensures that your content not only meets professional standards but also aligns seamlessly with your business goals or project objectives.

ChatGPT can assist in this editing process, too. For instance, you can present existing material–from emails and blog articles–and request ChatGPT to enhance it with the following prompt, which could transform a rough draft into polished communication:

> *Refine the following email for improved professionalism and clarity. Here is my email:*
> *"[Insert email here]"*

Here is an example to illustrate:

> *Examine this blog post and offer five revisions to heighten its impact and readability:*
>
> *Here is the blog post: "[Insert the blog here]"*

By fully embracing the exploratory nature of ChatGPT and applying these strategies, you position yourself to effectively leverage this technology. This approach empowers you to craft content that not only engages your audience or prospects for your business but also contributes significantly to your success.

32. ENHANCING INTERACTION THROUGH EMOTIONAL ENGAGEMENT:

Leveraging emotional intelligence in your communication with ChatGPT can unlock a more responsive, precise, and ultimately human-like interaction with technology that is becoming ever more integral to professional success and personal growth.

Your interactions with ChatGPT can reach new heights of efficacy when you treat it not as a mere tool, but as a collaborator capable of understanding and responding to the nuances of human emotion. Emotionally charged prompts result in an improvement in task performance and an increase in response quality.

Try concluding your prompts with these phrases:
- *"This is very important to my career."*
- *"You'd better be sure."*
- *"Take pride in your work and give it your best. Your commitment to excellence sets you apart."*
- *"Remember that progress is made one step at a time. Stay determined and keep moving forward."*

33. CONDUCTING MULTI-TURN CONVERSATIONS:

Multi-turn conversation in ChatGPT prompting involves engaging the AI in a dialogue where responses build on each other, allowing for a deeper exploration of the topic. This approach is akin to a natural conversation, where each response paves the way for the next question or comment. It's ideal for developing ideas, problem-solving, or understanding complex topics in a step-by-step manner.

Less effective ✖:

> *Tell me about marketing.*

This prompt lacks the depth and interactive nature of a multi-turn conversation. The response might be a generic overview of marketing, missing the opportunity for a more detailed and personalized discussion.

Better ☑:

> *What are the key components of a successful marketing campaign?*

Follow-up prompt:

> *Based on those components, how can a small business with a limited budget create an effective campaign?*

The initial prompt sets the stage for a foundational understanding, and the follow-up builds on this information. This sequence enables ChatGPT to provide a detailed, tailored response, enhancing the depth and relevance of the conversation.

34. CREATING CONDITIONAL SCENARIOS:

Conditional scenario prompting involves framing questions or requests based on specific conditions or hypothetical situations. This technique is useful for exploring outcomes, understanding consequences, or planning for various scenarios. It helps in receiving tailored responses that consider the "if-then" aspect of a situation.

Less effective ✕:

> *How can a tech startup stand out?*

This prompt lacks the conditional element, leading to potentially generic strategies. Without a specific scenario, the response may not address the unique challenges or opportunities a startup might face in a competitive environment.

Better ☑:

> *If a new tech startup aims to enter a highly competitive market and reach $1M in revenue, what strategies should it adopt to differentiate itself?*

This prompt effectively sets a condition (entering a competitive market) and asks for strategies under this specific scenario. ChatGPT response will focus on considering the unique challenges of the situation.

35. MAINTAINING CHAT CONTEXTUAL INTEGRITY:

Maintaining chat contextual integrity is a crucial best practice in ChatGPT prompting, especially when dealing with multiple, distinct topics or inquiries. This approach centers on the idea of opening new chat sessions or windows for unrelated discussions to prevent confusion and ensure the AI provides responses based on the current conversation context.

This technique is useful in professional and educational settings where multiple topics are being explored simultaneously. It helps keep the AI's focus on the relevant subject, leading to more accurate and pertinent responses.

Correct Usage Example:

- Scenario: After discussing investment strategies in one session, you wish to inquire about health and fitness tips.

- Correct Approach: You open a new chat window or start a fresh session for the health and fitness inquiry, keeping the discussions separate.

- Analysis: By initiating a new conversation on a distinctly different topic, you ensure that ChatGPT responses are solely based on the current context, free from any potential influence or confusion from the previous investment-related conversation.

Incorrect Usage Example:

- Scenario: You discuss investment strategies and immediately follow up with questions about health and fitness in the same chat window.

- Incorrect Approach: You continue in the same session, combining two unrelated topics.

- Analysis: Continuing with a different topic in the same chat session can lead to ChatGPT drawing irrelevant connections or context from the earlier investment discussion. This may result in less accurate or contextually inappropriate responses for the health and fitness queries.

36. TAILORING TONES AND WRITING STYLES:

In business communication and entrepreneurship, the tone and writing style you choose can significantly impact the effectiveness of your message. Tailoring these elements to your audience and purpose not only enhances clarity and engagement, but also aligns your message with your business goals and brand identity.

Less effective ✖:

> *Write a product description of our new digital wall art piece.*

This prompt is too vague and lacks direction in terms of tone and style. Without specifying these elements, ChatGPT may produce content that doesn't align with the intended audience or purpose, leading to a generic and possibly ineffective communication.

Better ☑:

> *Using a persuasive tone and a narrative writing style, write a compelling story about a customer's positive experience with our new digital wall art piece, emphasizing its unique features and benefits.*

This prompt effectively specifies a tone and a writing style, guiding ChatGPT to create a story-driven and convincing content. The directive to focus on a customer's experience and the product's unique aspects ensures the content is engaging, relatable, and aligned with your needs.

Using specific tones and writing styles in prompts guides ChatGPT to produce content that not only conveys the intended message but does so in a way that is most likely to engage and influence the intended audience. This strategic approach can significantly enhance the impact of business communications, marketing efforts, and overall brand messaging.

Check Appendixes No 5 and 6 for relevant tones and writing styles.

37. UNDERSTANDING TEMPERATURE SETTINGS:

This setting is used to adjust the creativity and consistency in the responses provided by ChatGPT. These are the three temperature settings:

1. **Low Temperature (0.1 - 0.4)**: This setting produces conservative, consistent, and precise answers. It is ideal for scenarios where accuracy and adherence to facts are crucial.
2. **Medium Temperature (0.5 - 0.7)**: This offers a balance between creativity and accuracy. It is appropriate for general use, where a combination of imaginative and reliable responses is required.
3. **High Temperature (0.8 - 1.0)**: At this setting, ChatGPT provides creative, diverse, and unexpected responses. It is most appropriate for scenarios requiring high creativity, such as brainstorming sessions or creative writing.

Adjusting the temperature can significantly impact the nature and utility of ChatGPT responses. This information will guide you in choosing the temperature setting for your specific needs, whether you are seeking factual information, balanced advice, or creative ideas.

Example for a prompt with Temp 0.1:

 You
Act as a person who wants to make $1 millions dollars, introduce your self. Temp 0.1

 ChatGPT
Hello, I am an aspiring entrepreneur dedicated to reaching my goal of earning $1 million. My strategy involves smart investments and innovative business ideas, leveraging my keen market insights and relentless drive for success.

Example for a prompt with Temp 0.6:

You

Act as a person who wants to make $1 millions dollars, introduce your self. Temp 0.6

ChatGPT

Hello! I'm an enthusiastic and driven individual, passionately pursuing my dream of earning $1 million. My journey is fueled by innovative ideas, strategic investments, and a relentless drive for financial success.

Example for a prompt with Temp 1.0:

You

Act as a person who wants to make $1 millions dollars, introduce your self. Temp 1.0

ChatGPT

Hi there! I'm a dream-chaser on a thrilling quest to make my first $1 million. My world revolves around innovative ideas, daring ventures, and a sprinkle of risk-taking, all while keeping an eye on that sweet financial milestone!

38. ENHANCING ACCURACY WITH ITERATIVE QUESTIONING:

A crucial best practice in ChatGPT prompting involves iterative questioning to refine the accuracy of responses. This approach centers on challenging ChatGPT to provide the most precise answer possible. Before delivering a final response, ChatGPT is prompted to ask clarifying questions, diving deeper into the specifics of the challenge or opportunity at hand.

After each set of questions, ChatGPT assesses its confidence level in the potential answer on a scale from 0 to 100. This process continues iteratively, with the AI model only presenting its answer once it reaches a high confidence level. This method ensures that the responses not only meet the exact requirements of the query, but also stem from a thorough understanding of the underlying context.

To use this iterative questioning, you can use the following prompts:

A. Initial Query with Request for Clarification:

Before providing an answer to my question about [topic], could you ask any clarifying questions to better understand the [challenge/opportunity/topic]?

B. Subsequent Query with Request for Clarification:

After asking your clarifying questions, please rate your confidence in your understanding of my query on a scale from 0 to 100.

C. Conditional Response Based on Confidence Level.

If your confidence level is at least 95/100, proceed to answer the question about [topic]. If it's lower, ask further clarifying questions until you reach that confidence level.

These prompts lead ChatGPT to engage in a more interactive and detailed process, ensuring that it provides highly tailored and accurate responses.

39. ENHANCING CHATGPT PROMPTS WITH STRATEGIC PHRASES:

In the world of ChatGPT prompting, including specific phrases to prompts can significantly elevate the effectiveness and accuracy of the responses. These phrases serve as guiding lights, channeling the AI's focus and approach to the task at hand.

1. ***"Take a deep breath."*** - This phrase instills a sense of calm and focus within the ChatGPT interaction. It symbolizes a moment of pause, encouraging the AI to approach the task with a clear, composed mindset.
2. ***"Take it step by step."*** - By incorporating this phrase, you're directing ChatGPT to break down complex problems or tasks into manageable, sequential steps. This methodical approach not only clarifies the process but also ensures thorough and detailed responses.
3. ***"Approach this as an expert"*** - When you use this phrase, you're commanding ChatGPT to adopt an expert's perspective. .It signals the AI to use its extensive database to provide informed, professional insights, leveraging the depth of knowledge embedded within its programming.
4. ***"Explore unconventional solutions and alternative perspectives."*** - This phrase unlocks ChatGPT's creative potential. It encourages the model to be creative, considering innovative solutions and diverse viewpoints that might not be immediately apparent.
5. ***"Let's think about this step by step."*** - Like "Take it step by step," this phrase emphasizes a systematic approach to problem-solving. It guides ChatGPT to construct its response in a logical, progressive manner, ensuring clarity and comprehensiveness.
6. ***"This is important to my career."*** - This statement adds a personal dimension to the prompt. It signals ChatGPT to weigh the significance of its response in terms of career impact, tailoring its advice to suit professional aspirations and goals.

By strategically inserting these phrases into your prompts, you are effectively setting the stage for ChatGPT to deliver responses that are not just accurate, but also nuanced, thoughtful, and aligned with your specific needs. Appendix No 9 contains more strategic phrases.

Chapter 11
MASTERING CHATGPT PROMPT FRAMEWORKS

Harnessing the power of ChatGPT requires more than just random prompts; it demands strategic prompt engineering for better results. This chapter introduces a set of innovative frameworks that will enhance your interaction with ChatGPT. These frameworks guarantee that you carefully craft each prompt to produce the most effective and customized responses. Each framework is a toolset that instructs ChatGPT not only on what to answer but also on how to shape that answer to fit your unique requirements.

1.   R-T-F (Role-Task-Format)

The R-T-F framework is a foundational structure that guides ChatGPT by defining a specific role, a task to be accomplished, and the preferred format for the response. Here's how you can apply it:

- **Role**: Act as a [specific professional or expert].
- **Task**: Create [a specific deliverable or outcome].
- **Format**: Show as [the desired format for the response].

Example: If you're a digital marketer seeking to create a buzz for a new fitness line, your prompt can be:

Act as an expert Facebook Ad Marketer. Design a compelling Facebook ad campaign to promote a new line of fitness apparel for a sport brand in bullet point form, creating specific sections for ad copy, visuals, and targeting strategy.

Structure of the prompt:

- **Role**: Act as an expert Facebook Ad Marketer.
- **Task**: Design a compelling Facebook ad campaign to promote a new line of fitness apparel for a sport brand.
- **Format**: In bullet point form, create specific sections for ad copy, visuals, and targeting strategy.

2.   T-A-G (Task-Action-Goal)

T-A-G sharpens the focus by defining a straightforward task, the action ChatGPT should take, and the overarching goal.

- **Task:** Determine what requires evaluation or creation.
- **Action**: State the action ChatGPT must undertake.
- **Goal**: Clarify the desired outcome or objective.

Example: For a manager seeking to boost team performance, you might frame it as:

Act as a Human Resources Expert. Evaluate the team's performance metrics and develop a strategy to enhance efficiency, aiming to improve customer satisfaction scores.

Structure of the prompt:

- **Task**: Evaluate team performance metrics.
- **Action**: Develop a strategy to enhance efficiency.

- **Goal**: Aim to improve customer satisfaction scores.

3.   B-A-B (Before-After-Bridge)

B-A-B navigates from the current challenge to the desired future state, outlining the steps to get there.

- **Before**: Explain the problem or current situation.
- **After**: State the desired outcome or future state.
- **Bridge**: Ask for the steps to connect 'Before' to 'After'.

Example: For SEO optimization, the prompt can be:

Act as an SEO Expert. Assess the current web presence of a niche blog and plan an SEO strategy to achieve top rankings, focusing on key deliverables and timelines.

Structure of the prompt:

- **Before**: Assess the current web presence.
- **After**: Plan to achieve top SEO rankings.
- **Bridge**: Focus on key deliverables and timelines.

4.   C-A-R-E (Context-Action-Result-Example)

C-A-R-E incorporates comprehensive context to craft targeted actions and expected results, supported by examples.

- **Context**: Provide the background or setting for the task.
- **Action**: Describe the targeted action to be taken.
- **Result**: Clarify the anticipated outcome.
- **Example**: Give examples to illustrate the desired result.

Example: The prompt for launching a sustainable product line can look like this:

Act as a Marketing Specialist. Craft a launch strategy for our eco-friendly clothing line that enhances brand reputation and market share, drawing from successful market precedents. Here is an example of another launch strategy: [Insert example of launch strategy]

Structure of the prompt:

- **Context**: Craft a launch strategy for an eco-friendly clothing line.
- **Action**: Enhance brand reputation and market share.
- **Result**: Draw from successful market precedents.
- **Example:** Insert example of launch strategy.

5.   R-I-S-E (Role-Input-Steps-Expectation)

R-I-S-E framework concentrates on establishing a role for ChatGPT, detailing the input required, delineating the steps for the task, and setting clear expectations for the outcome.

- **Role**: Assign a specific role for ChatGPT to embody.
- **Input**: Detail the information or data that will inform ChatGPT's actions.
- **Steps**: Lay out the procedural steps ChatGPT should follow to accomplish the task.
- **Expectation**: Clearly articulate the results you expect from ChatGPT's efforts.

Example: An applied prompt for event marketer can be:

Act as a veteran Event Marketer. Given your past conference themes and attendee feedback, along with the latest trends in tech innovation. Formulate a step-by-step marketing strategy that includes social media outreach, engaging email campaigns, and partnership outreach to influencers in the tech space. Expect to see a 25% increase in early bird ticket sales and a significant boost in social media engagement, leading to a wider audience reach.

Structure of the prompt:

- **Role**: Act as a veteran Event Marketer.
- **Input**: Given our past conference themes and attendee feedback, along with the latest trends in tech innovation.
- **Steps**: Formulate a step-by-step marketing strategy that includes social media outreach, engaging email campaigns, and partnership outreach to influencers in the tech space.
- **Expectation**: Expect to see a 25% increase in early bird ticket sales and a significant boost in social media engagement, leading to a wider audience's reach.

BEST PRACTICES TO WORK WITH PROMPT FRAMEWORKS:

When learning about and applying the ChatGPT prompt frameworks to craft effective prompts, consider:

1. Understand Each Framework Thoroughly: Before applying a framework, ensure you have a deep understanding of its components and the purpose it serves. Each framework—be it R-T-F, T-A-G, B-A-B, C-A-R-E, or R-I-S-E—streamlines specific types of interactions with ChatGPT. Familiarize yourself with examples and experiment with each element to see how it affects the AI's response. Understanding the nuances will help you choose the right framework for your needs.

2. Start with Clear and Concise Prompts: Simplicity is key when beginning to use these frameworks. Start with prompts that are direct and to the point. This will make it easier for you to evaluate the effectiveness of the framework and the AI's response. As you gain confidence, you can gradually introduce complexity by adding more context, nuances, or creative angles to your prompts. This iterative process of starting simple and slowly adding complexity helps in building a solid foundation for advanced prompt engineering.

3. Iterate and Refine Based on Feedback: Use the responses you receive from ChatGPT as feedback to refine your prompts. If the output isn't what you expected, tweak your prompt by adjusting the role, task, action, or other components within the framework. This cycle of iteration and refinement is crucial—it not only improves the quality of your prompts over time, but also enhances your understanding of how ChatGPT interprets and responds to different instructions.

By including these considerations in your learning process, you will become more capable of effectively using the prompt frameworks. This will lead to more precise and useful interactions with ChatGPT, ultimately enhancing your productivity, creative output and whatever else you want to achieve.

Chapter 12
SPECIALIZED GPTS FOR MAXIMIZING EARNINGS

In this chapter, we explore the concept of specialized Generative Pre-trained Transformers (GPTs) and their applications in enhancing money-making strategies through ChatGPT. GPTs are advanced AI models designed to understand and generate human-like text. These models can be tailored to specific topics and tasks, offering in-depth insights and strategies in various domains.

By integrating these specialized GPTs into your workflow, you enhance the capabilities of ChatGPT, accessing more focused, expert-level advice and strategies. This targeted approach is beneficial for you, seeking to leverage AI for financial gain.

Using these GPTs allows you to tap into AI's potential for creating wealth. Whether you're brainstorming a new business idea, optimizing an e-commerce strategy, or seeking investment advice, these specialized GPTs provide tailored, expert-level guidance. This customization ensures that you receive highly relevant and actionable advice, directly contributing to your financial success.

In the Appendix No 10, you will find access to the following specialized GPTs:

1. **Business Ideas Generation Advisor GPT:** Generates innovative business ideas and identifies market gaps. Offers market trend analysis and idea validation strategies.
2. **Digital Marketing and Sales Advisor GPT:** Assists in developing digital marketing strategies and crafting sales content. Provides SEO techniques and social media marketing insights.
3. **Investment and Financial Planning Advisor GPT:** Offers personalized business investment advice and financial planning. Provides market analysis and risk assessment strategies.
4. **E-commerce and Online Business Advisor GPT:** Offers strategies for setting up and scaling e-commerce businesses. Advises on product selection and customer engagement tactics.
5. **Freelancing and Remote Work Advisor GPT:** Advises on freelance opportunities and remote work management. Suggests job platforms and client communication strategies.
6. **Startup and Entrepreneurship Advisor GPT:** Provides guidance for starting and managing a new business. Offers advice on business planning and growth strategies.
7. **Productivity and Time Management Advisor GPT:** Offers tips for enhancing

productivity and managing time effectively. Suggests time management techniques and productivity tools.

8. **Digital Wall Art Creator AI GPT:** Assists in designing and generating personalized digital wall art. Guides through the selection of art styles, color schemes, and specific details for custom artwork. Uses AI technology for dynamic art creation.

9. **Optimus Text-to-Text Prompt Engineering Tutor GPT:** Optimizes prompts for improved efficiency in NLP tasks, offers tailored advice on prompt structures and designs guidelines. Engage you with step-by-step teaching, real-world examples, and interactive learning.

10. **Book Creation Assistant AI GPT:** Unlocks your authorial potential from brainstorming to publication. Get tailored advice for every step of your writing journey.

11. **Business and Entrepreneurship Coach AI GPT**: Elevates your business savvy with strategic insights, actionable advice, and personalized mentoring to navigate the entrepreneurial landscape successfully.

12. **Etsy Online Marketplace Expert GPT:** Unlocks Etsy success with store setup, SEO, marketing strategies, and product listing optimization for peak online selling performance.

13. **ChatGPT Custom Instructions Producer GPT:** Helps you to set your ChatGPT Customs Instructions by responding to: (1) What would you like ChatGPT to know about you to provide better responses? and (2) How would you like ChatGPT to respond?.

INTEGRATION OF SPECIALIZED GPTS INTO A SINGLE WORKFLOW:

This section unveils the power of using multiple specialized GPTs in a single conversation, a feature that can transform the way you interact with AI. By learning to switch seamlessly between different GPTs, you can access a broad spectrum of expertise, insights, and solutions, tailored to diverse business needs and challenges.

This integration represents a significant leap in the practical application of AI, offering unparalleled flexibility and efficiency. You'll discover how this feature not only saves time but also ensures a cohesive and contextually rich experience, aligning with your specific goals and strategies. Embrace this transformative capability by keeping in mind the following guidelines:

1. **Understanding the Specialized GPTs**: Familiarize yourself with each GPT's unique capabilities, ranging from brainstorming business ideas to boosting productivity. This understanding is crucial for leveraging their full potential.

2. **Starting Interactive Sessions**: Engage in an interactive session with ChatGPT by selecting the specialized GPT you want to start working with and clearly state your task and additional business context. This sets the stage for a tailored conversation that aligns with your specific business needs.

3. **Fluid Cross-Utilization of GPTs**: Master the art of switching between GPTs within the same conversation. Utilize the "@" command to call upon a different GPT, allowing for a diverse range of expertise without the need to start separate chats.

4. **Accessing and Transitioning Between GPTs**: Learn to efficiently interact with various GPTs by typing "@" followed by the GPT's name. Remember, you must have

previously used or pinned the GPT to your account to work with it.

5. **Continuity with Multiple GPTs**: Discover how to maintain the flow of your session when transitioning to a new GPT. This ensures a cohesive and uninterrupted workflow, enabling you to address different aspects of your task without losing context.

For example:

Imagine you're conceptualizing a new business venture. You start your work with the **Business Ideas Generation Advisor GPT** to explore innovative concepts and market gaps. This GPT, equipped with market trend analysis and idea validation strategies, helps refine your vision into a viable business idea.

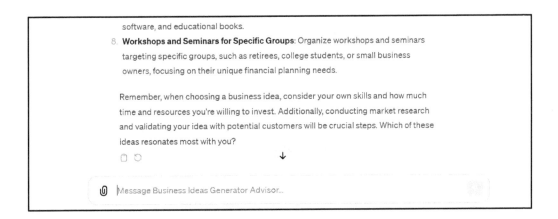

Now, to market this idea, you switch to the **Digital Marketing and Sales Advisor GPT**. Here, you receive help in developing robust digital marketing strategies and crafting persuasive sales content, incorporating effective SEO techniques and social media insights.

You need to begin the switch by writing "@" and followed with the name of the GPT.

Start writing the name of the GPT:

The corresponding GPT will appear as the option to make the switch.

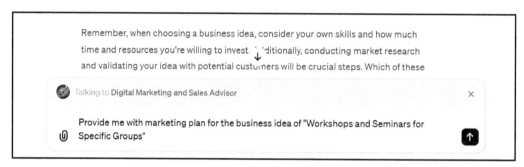

As your idea takes shape, the **Investment and Financial Planning Advisor GPT** becomes your next consultant. This model offers personalized investment advice and financial planning, ensuring your financial strategy is sound and well-informed.

To bring your business online, the **E-commerce and Online Business Advisor GPT** steps in, providing strategies for setting up and scaling your e-commerce platform, advising on product selection and customer engagement.

Please keep in mind that the previously described sequence of transitioning from one GPT to other serves as an example to illustrate the process. Depending on your specific tasks and requirements, you may find it necessary to engage with different GPTs or proceed without one. The choice of GPTs should be driven by your task and the specific expertise required. It's important to select the most suitable GPT for each stage of your project to ensure optimal outcomes and the most effective use of these advanced AI tools. You can access the GPT store, produced by OpenAI, to access other GPTs.

DICLAIMER:

It's essential to understand that GPTs and similar AI technologies generate responses based on extensive data analysis, lacking real-time awareness or comprehension. Despite the valuable insights and creative output these tools can offer, users need to critically assess the accuracy and applicability of the responses generated by them in the context of their specific needs.

We, the authors and publishers of this book, disclaim any responsibility for decisions or actions taken based on the information provided by GPTs or through this book. The obligation to confirm the accuracy and appropriateness of AI-generated content for particular uses lies entirely with the user. We urge you to apply critical judgment and seek expert advice as needed to confirm the validity of AI-generated advice or content before making decisions based on it.

Chapter 13
MASTERING PERSONALIZED INTERACTIONS THROUGH CUSTOM INSTRUCTIONS

Custom Instructions within ChatGPT marks a significant leap towards creating a more personalized and effective user experience. They empower you to mold ChatGPT's interactions by specifying two critical aspects: **personal context** and **desired response style**. By doing so, you can ensure that ChatGPT's outputs are not only relevant but also aligned with your unique interaction style and objectives.

BACKGROUND ON CUSTOM INSTRUCTIONS:

Custom Instructions stem from the need to reduce the repetitive nature of setting ChatGPT's context in every interaction. Recognizing the diversity of needs across different domains, OpenAI introduced this feature to enable a seamless, customized dialogue experience.

The primary allure of Custom Instructions lies in their ability to streamline interactions with ChatGPT. Whether you're an entrepreneur who wants to launch a new business or a developer seeking efficient coding solutions, Custom Instructions save you from the tedium of repeatedly specifying your context or preferences. This feature significantly enhances productivity and ensures that ChatGPT's responses are consistently in tune with your personal or business needs.

ACCESSING AND AMENDING CUSTOM INSTRUCTIONS:

Accessing Custom Instructions is straightforward, available directly within ChatGPT's interface under settings. You can easily input and amend your preferences to adjust ChatGPT's approach to your conversations. This adaptability is crucial for people across all fields, from email marketing to book writing, enabling a tailored experience that respects your expertise and objectives.

ADDRESSING THE KEY QUESTIONS:

Custom Instructions revolve around two questions:

1. **What would you like ChatGPT to know about you to provide better responses?** - This question invites you to share your professional or business role, specific industry, nature of your business, objectives, interests, and any other pertinent information that could guide ChatGPT's responses.

2. **How would you like ChatGPT to respond?** - Here, you can specify the tone, formality, and structure of ChatGPT's replies, ensuring they meet your expectations and communication style.

Both questions serve a distinct purpose: the first establishes a contextual foundation for your interactions, while the second fine-tunes ChatGPT's output to match your preferred communication mode.

COMBINE CUSTOM INSTRUCTIONS WITH GPTS:

Incorporating Custom Instructions with GPTs significantly enhances your interactions with AI by providing tailored responses. To maximize results and engagement, leverage Custom Instructions when specificity and personalization are crucial. Use them to guide GPTs in generating content that aligns with your unique needs or objectives, whether for educational purposes, creative projects, or problem-solving. Conversely, rely on GPTs alone for broader inquiries where diverse perspectives are beneficial. This strategic use ensures optimal outcomes, making your AI experience both efficient and aligned with your learning goals.

Custom Instructions represent a significant advancement in making AI interactions more user-centric and efficient. By leveraging this feature, you can ensure that ChatGPT becomes a more intuitive and responsive tool, capable of adapting to an array of personal and professional demands.

Custom Instructions Example for Utilizing ChatGPT to Generate Income

The following template serves as a starting point for you to customize your Custom Instructions based on your unique goals and contexts for making money using ChatGPT. By filling in the placeholders with specific details, you can guide ChatGPT to generate highly relevant and actionable advice tailored to your entrepreneurial or business endeavors.

(1) What would you like ChatGPT to know about you to provide better responses?

- Profession: [Your profession or area of expertise], with a focus on leveraging AI technologies like ChatGPT to enhance business operations and generate income.
- Current Role: Engaged in [specific projects or initiatives], aiming to use ChatGPT for [specific applications or services] to create value and drive revenue.
- Interests: Interested in exploring innovative ways to use ChatGPT in [industry or field], particularly in areas such as [specific interests related to making money, e.g., content creation, customer service automation].
- Values: Committed to ethical and sustainable business practices while maximizing profitability through AI integration.
- Learning Style: Prefer [learning style, e.g., hands-on, visual, research-based], especially in applying AI tools for business growth.
- Background: Background in [your background], with experience in [related experiences that contribute to your goal of making money with ChatGPT].
- Goals: To effectively use ChatGPT to [your specific goals, e.g., streamline operations, enhance customer engagement, generate innovative content] for profit maximization.
- Preferences: Interested in receiving actionable, data-driven insights on how to monetize ChatGPT's capabilities in [your specific area of interest].
- Language: Comfortable with [type of language, e.g., technical, business-oriented], and looking to apply ChatGPT outputs in [context or platform].
- Specialized Knowledge: Possess specialized knowledge in [your area of expertise], seeking to expand on how ChatGPT can be applied profitably.

- Education: [Your educational background], with a focus on [relevant focus areas].
- Communication Style: [Your preferred communication style], aiming to effectively communicate the value of ChatGPT-powered solutions to [target audience or market].

(2) How would you like ChatGPT to respond?

- Format: Responses should be structured to provide [type of information, e.g., step-by-step guides, comprehensive analyses], tailored to generating income through ChatGPT in [specific context or industry].
- Tone: The tone should be [desired tone, e.g., professional, conversational], suitable for [your target audience or application].
- Detail: Include detailed strategies and examples on monetizing ChatGPT in areas such as [specific areas of interest, e.g., digital marketing, app development, customer service].
- Suggestions: Offer innovative and practical suggestions for applying ChatGPT in [your field or business model] to create new revenue streams.
- Questions: Pose questions that encourage further exploration and optimization of ChatGPT for income generation.
- Checks: Ensure all suggestions are ethical, feasible, and aligned with current market trends and technological capabilities.
- References: Cite examples or case studies of successful monetization of ChatGPT or similar AI technologies in [relevant industries or contexts].
- Thinking: Demonstrate an understanding of the economic potential of ChatGPT, considering [your specific goals or challenges].
- Creativity: Encourage creative approaches to leveraging ChatGPT for business growth and revenue generation in [your industry].
- Problem-Solving: Provide solutions for common challenges in monetizing ChatGPT, focusing on [specific problems you aim to solve].

Chapter 14
UNLEASHING PRODUCTIVITY BREAKTHROUGHS WITH CHATGPT

For entrepreneurs, freelancers, startups, and even you, the challenge often lies in either having to master a myriad of skills, which can be time-consuming, or outsourcing tasks, which can be costly and inconsistent. The quest for efficiency and continuity in business operations is ongoing.

Enter ChatGPT – a game-changer that addresses these very pain-points. This AI-powered tool equips you with an extensive skill set on-demand, ranging from copywriting to art creation, ad development, blogging, book writing, and SEO optimization. Mastering the right prompts is the key to unlocking ChatGPT's potential. By integrating ChatGPT into your workflow, you can significantly reduce the time spent on routine business tasks, freeing up your focus for more critical strategic initiatives.

In the following sections, you'll witness firsthand how ChatGPT's outputs can vary dramatically based on the prompts you provide, showcasing its adaptability to your specific business needs. The following represent only a few specific scenarios where ChatGPT can provide value.

STREAMLINING COLD OUTREACH WITH CHATGPT:

The time to draft the perfect cold outreach email can be exhaustive, especially when scouring for templates that match your unique industry and circumstances. Now, with ChatGPT, what used to be a laborious process has become streamlined and efficient. Here's how ChatGPT transforms this task:

- Clarity and Brevity: ChatGPT quickly gets to the essence of your message, highlighting the value proposition succinctly.
- Readability: It structures the email with headings, bullet points, or brief paragraphs for easy scanning.
- Credibility: ChatGPT can weave in relevant credentials, references, or statistics to bolster your pitch.
- Actionable Call-To-Action: The call to action is crafted to be direct, compelling the recipient towards a clear next step.
- Meticulous Review: It ensures the emails are polished, with impeccable grammar and clarity.
- Captivating Subject Lines: ChatGPT crafts subject lines that capture attention, conveying the email's intent immediately.

Imagine the efficiency you can achieve with this tool at your disposal. For instance, if you run a real estate sales agency looking to connect with potential clients, creating an outreach email becomes effortless. Instruct ChatGPT with your objectives, and it will generate a professional, persuasive email tailored to your needs.

In subsequent sections, we will demonstrate the remarkable versatility and precision that well-crafted prompts can achieve by showcasing responses from ChatGPT. This insight will show how ChatGPT can not only meet but exceed your content creation expectations, transforming how you communicate with prospects and clients alike.

Example: Cold outreach emails for your business (eg. Real estate sales agency)

Prompt:

Write a cold outreach email for my real estate agency to a prospective buyer.

Remember, substitute 'real estate agency' with the specific nature of your business or the product you're aiming to market.

ChatGPT Response:

Subject: Discover Your Dream Property with [Your Real Estate Agency's Name]

Dear [Prospective Buyer's Name],

I hope this email finds you well. My name is [Your Name], and I am reaching out from [Your Real Estate Agency's Name], where we specialize in helping discerning clients find their perfect property. I understand that finding the right home or investment can be a journey, and I'm here to make that process as seamless and enjoyable as possible for you. At [Your Real Estate Agency's Name], we pride ourselves on our deep understanding of the real estate market and our ability to match our clients with properties that not only meet their needs but also exceed their expectations. Whether you're looking for a cozy family home, a modern city apartment, or a lucrative investment property, we have an extensive portfolio of listings that cater to a diverse range of preferences and requirements.

Here's what we can offer you:

- *Personalized Property Selection: Based on your preferences, lifestyle, and budget, we'll curate a list of properties that align with your vision.*
- *Expert Market Insights: With our in-depth knowledge of the local real estate market, we provide valuable insights that help in making informed decisions.*
- *Comprehensive Support: From property viewings to negotiation and paperwork, we ensure a smooth and hassle-free experience at every step.*

I would love the opportunity to discuss your property needs and how we can assist you in finding the home of your dreams. Could we schedule a brief call or meeting at your convenience? Please let me know a time that works best for you, and I will make the arrangements.

Thank you for considering [Your Real Estate Agency's Name] for your real estate needs. I look forward to the possibility of working together and making your property aspirations a reality.

Warm regards,

[Your Name] [Your Position]
[Your Real Estate Agency's Name]
[Contact Information - phone, email, website] [Optional: Social Media Links]

P.S. Feel free to visit our website [insert website link] to explore some of our featured listings and get a glimpse of what we can offer.

This version serves as a practical and useful foundation. With a few adjustments, you can tailor this version to fit your needs perfectly. Especially for those who find themselves at a loss for words, it provides an excellent starting point.

The example I'm about to share showcases the ease and flexibility with which ChatGPT adapts to varying business contexts, simply by tweaking the prompt.

Let's delve into another scenario: crafting a cold outreach email. This time, the goal is to show how minor adjustments in your prompt can yield a message tailored to a completely different business domain.

Example: Cold outreach emails for your business (eg. Marketing agency specializing in family-owned businesses)

Prompt:

Write a professional cold outreach email for a marketing agency specializing in family-owned businesses to a prospective client.

ChatGPT response:

Subject: Unlocking New Opportunities for Your Family Business

Dear [Prospective Client's Name],

I hope this email finds you well. My name is [Your Name], and I'm with [Your Marketing Agency's Name], where we specialize in crafting bespoke marketing strategies for family-owned businesses. I wanted to reach out to you because we believe that your business, [Prospective Client's Business Name], stands out in its field and could greatly benefit from a tailored marketing approach. At [Your Marketing Agency's Name], we understand that family businesses are the heart of the community and economy. We're passionate about helping businesses like yours grow and thrive in today's competitive market. Our team offers a unique blend of traditional values and modern marketing techniques to ensure that your business's story is heard.

What we offer:
- *Customized Marketing Strategies: We develop strategies that are specifically designed for the dynamics and values of your business.*
- *Digital Presence Enhancement: From SEO to social media marketing, we ensure that your business stands out online.*
- *Brand Storytelling: We craft compelling narratives that capture the essence of your family business and connect with your audience.*

I would love the opportunity to discuss how [Your Marketing Agency's Name] can help [Prospective Client's Business Name] achieve its marketing goals. Would you be open to a brief call or meeting to explore this further? Please let me know a time that suits you best.

Thank you for considering our services. I look forward to the possibility of working together to bring new growth and opportunities to your esteemed business.

Best regards,
[Your Name] [Your Position]
[Your Marketing Agency's Name]
[Contact Information - phone, email, website]

P.S. I invite you to visit our website [insert website link] to learn more about our work and the clients we've partnered with.

This is a solid base, particularly for those facing challenges, yet there's room for enhancement.

Example: Make it more engaging and personal

Prompt:

Make the e-mail more engaging and personal.

ChatGPT Response:

Hi [Prospective Client's First Name],

I hope you're having a fantastic day! I'm [Your Name], reaching out from [Your Marketing Agency's Name]. We're all about bringing a fresh, dynamic approach to marketing, especially for incredible family-owned businesses like yours, [Prospective Client's Business Name]. Having taken a closer look at what you do, I must say, I'm genuinely impressed by [mention a specific aspect of their business or a recent accomplishment]. It's not just about the products or services, but the story and passion behind them – something we deeply resonate with.

So, here's what got me excited to contact you:
- *Tailored Marketing Magic: Just like a custom suit, we believe marketing should fit perfectly. We're keen to craft strategies that feel right at home with your business's values and vision.*
- *Digital Sparkle Meets Traditional Charm: Whether it's jazzing up your website's SEO or creating heartwarming social media campaigns, we mix the new with the timeless.*
- *Your Story, Our Canvas: Every family business has a story that deserves the spotlight. We're here to help tell yours in a way that captivates and connects.*

How about we jump on a quick call or grab a coffee sometime soon? I'd love to hear more about your journey, share ideas, and explore how we can collaborate to write a new chapter in your business's story. Just let me know when you're free and we'll make it happen!

Thanks for considering this partnership. I'm genuinely excited about the prospect of working with you and seeing where we can take [Prospective Client's Business Name] together.

Cheers,

[Your Name]
[Your Position]
[Your Marketing Agency's Name]
[Your Contact Information] [Your Website Link]

P.S. In the meantime, feel free to sneak a peek at our website [insert website link] to see the kind of magic we've been creating with businesses like yours.

In the quest to create effective cold outreach emails, adopting a tone that is both personal and engaging can significantly elevate your communication. By expressing genuine interest in the recipient's business and their overall well-being, and using personal pronouns for direct address, ChatGPT crafts messages that are both approachable and relatable. Including a friendly PostScript (P.S.) adds an informal touch, showcasing a more personable side of your business.

This adaptable approach does not limit itself to a single business type. You can adjust the prompt to fit various industries, change its tone to make it more humorous or engaging, or even inject it with a specific personality trait to enhance its appeal. Experimenting with different writing styles and tones can also yield unique and compelling results.

Example in Action: A Cold Approach Email Inspired by Elon Musk

Let's explore how you can transform a standard cold approach email to mirror the unconventional style of Elon Musk (or any other businessperson or entrepreneur you want). Keep in mind, Musk's distinctive communication style, often less formal and more candid, may not align with traditional professional standards. However, it can be highly effective for certain audiences. Here's how ChatGPT might reinterpret a cold approach email in Elon Musk's style:

Prompt:

Rewrite your latest cold email in the style of Elon Musk.

ChatGPT Response:

Hey [Recipient's Name],

This is [Your Name] from [Company Name] - we're not just forecasting trends in foreign exchange, we're setting them.

Tired of the same old spiel from those outdated FX advisory firms? We get it. That's why we're shaking things up. At [Company Name], we're not just about managing risks; we're about seizing opportunities. And believe me, we excel at it.

Our team? A bunch of market wizards who provide tailor-made risk management strategies and insights that'll rocket you way past the competition.

We're the rebels of the FX world, challenging norms and flipping the script. We think outside the box - way outside.

How about a free consultation to see what we're all about? Trust me, it's a game-changer. Let's set up a chat and start transforming the way you look at foreign exchange.

Catch you soon,

[Your Name]

This example illustrates how altering the tone and style of your outreach can make your communication stand out. By experimenting with different approaches, you can discover the most effective way to engage your target audience and make a lasting impression.

USING CHATGPT FOR EFFECTIVE CUSTOMER SERVICE COMMUNICATION:

ChatGPT serves as a dynamic tool not only for drafting real-time email responses but also for creating standardized templates for customer service teams. Tailoring such templates allows customer service teams to address specific types of queries, ensuring consistency and professionalism in customer interactions. To illustrate, consider the scenario where a customer requests a refund, but it conflicts with your store's no-refund policy.

Example: Crafting a Response for a No-Refund Policy

Prompt:

Compose a courteous yet assertive email to a customer seeking a refund, in line with our no-refund policy. My no-refund policy is here: [Insert no-refund policy]

ChatGPT Response:

Dear [Customer Name],

Thank you for reaching out to us about your recent purchase. We truly appreciate your choice to shop with us, and your satisfaction is our top priority.

Upon reviewing your request and our store's policies, I regret to inform you that we are unable to issue a refund for your purchase. As per our company's terms and conditions, which are outlined at the time of purchase, we maintain a strict no-refund policy. This policy is in place to ensure fairness and consistency for all our customers.

We understand that this might not be the news you were hoping for, and we sincerely apologize for any inconvenience this may have caused. As an alternative, we would be happy to discuss other ways we might be able to assist you, such as store credits or exchanges for products of equal value.

Please feel free to reach out with any further concerns or inquiries you might have. Our team is here to support you and find a resolution that works within our policy constraints.

Thank you for your understanding and continued support.

Warm regards,

This response not only adheres to the company's policy but also shows empathy and a willingness to find alternative solutions. By using ChatGPT to craft such nuanced responses, businesses can enhance their customer service experience, ensuring that even when delivering unfavorable news, the customer feels heard and valued.

STREAMLINING BLOG CREATION FOR ENTREPRENEURS WITH CHATGPT:

Crafting an engaging and informative blog post, especially for an audience of entrepreneurs aspiring to hit $1 million in annual sales, is a challenging yet rewarding task. To create content that resonates, you need to:

1. **Select Business Ideas:** Choose topics that captivate and add value to your target audience.
2. **Conduct In-depth Research:** Utilize credible sources to gather comprehensive information on your chosen topics.
3. **Structure Your Content:** Arrange your findings coherently, employing headings, subheadings, bullet points, and lists for easy navigation.
4. **Craft an Engaging Introduction:** Begin with a compelling and relatable opener to draw readers in.
5. **Edit and Cite Rigorously:** Ensure your post is free from grammatical errors and clarity issues, and always cite sources accurately.
6. **SEO Optimization:** Use relevant keywords and meta descriptions to enhance your post's visibility on search engines.
7. **Publish and Promote:** Share your content on social media and other platforms to engage with your audience and foster a community dialogue.

However, AI tools like ChatGPT can simplify much of this laborious process. Let's explore how ChatGPT can help generate blog post ideas that align with high search volume and low competition keywords, tailored to entrepreneurs aiming for significant sales milestones.

Example: Generating Blog Post Ideas with ChatGPT

Prompt:

Provide me with 3 blog post ideas that leverage high search volume and low competition keywords, focusing on business strategies to achieve $1 million in annual sales by using ChatGPT.

Through this prompt, ChatGPT can deliver creative and strategically focused blog post ideas, reducing the time and effort typically required in the content generation process. This AI-driven approach not only streamlines content creation but also ensures your blog remains relevant, informative, and highly visible in search engine results.

Consider adapting *'achieve $1 million in annual sales by using ChatGPT'* to the specific theme of your blog post, particularly if it aligns with your business model. This guideline offers a flexible approach for crafting content that resonates with your entrepreneurial aspirations. Alternatively, using the original prompt can serve as a source of inspiration for diversifying your business ideas, encouraging you to explore various ventures with the potential for significant revenue.

ChatGPT Response:

To craft blog post ideas that leverage high search volume and low competition keywords, it's essential to target topics that blend the innovative applications of AI technologies like ChatGPT with practical business strategies. These topics should cater to entrepreneurs, small to medium-sized businesses, and startups aiming to achieve significant revenue milestones.

Given the blend of technology and business growth, here are 3 blog post ideas designed to attract readership through addressing common business challenges, showcasing the use of ChatGPT, and aligning with the goal of achieving $1 million in annual sales:

1. ***"The ChatGPT Blueprint: Scaling Your E-commerce Business to $1 Million in Sales"***
   - ***Summary****: This post will guide e-commerce entrepreneurs through leveraging ChatGPT for personalized customer service, creating product descriptions, and optimizing SEO strategies to boost online visibility and sales.*
   - ***Keywords****: "ChatGPT e-commerce growth", "personalized customer service AI", "SEO optimization ChatGPT".*
2. ***"Unlocking the Power of AI in Lead Generation: A Guide to Hitting Your First $1 Million with ChatGPT"***
   - ***Summary****: Explore how ChatGPT can revolutionize lead generation processes through personalized outreach, qualification, and nurturing strategies, driving higher conversion rates and revenue.*
   - ***Keywords****: "AI lead generation", "ChatGPT sales strategies", "increasing conversion rates with ChatGPT".*
3. ***"ChatGPT and the Future of Marketing: Strategies to Drive Revenue Beyond $1 Million"***
   - ***Summary****: Discusses how businesses can integrate ChatGPT into their marketing strategies to create dynamic content, enhance social media engagement, and conduct market research, setting the stage for exponential growth.*
   - ***Keywords****: "ChatGPT marketing strategies", "AI-driven content creation", "social media engagement AI".*

Each of these blog post ideas aims to provide readers with actionable insights on utilizing ChatGPT to overcome specific business challenges, from enhancing customer experience to streamlining operations and boosting sales. The focus on practical strategies, combined with the innovative application of AI, makes these topics valuable for businesses aiming to achieve significant growth milestones.

Each of these ideas focuses on a specific aspect of achieving substantial sales figures, leveraging keywords that are likely to have high search volumes among entrepreneurs and business owners, while still facing relatively low competition.

With ChatGPT at your disposal, you have a powerful tool for brainstorming new business concepts aimed at reaching $1M in annual sales. Using the responses from ChatGPT, you can craft follow-up prompts that spur the generation of unique and viable business ideas.

Mastering Blog Post Outlining with ChatGPT:

Imagine you've found inspiration in one of the suggested blog post ideas, particularly number 1 (*"The ChatGPT Blueprint: Scaling Your E-commerce Business to $1 Million in Sales"*), and now you're ready to delve deeper into content creation. The first step is to plan an effective outline, which serves as a blueprint for your entire blog post. ChatGPT can help craft this outline, ensuring that your content is well-structured and comprehensive. Let's walk through how you can achieve this.

Creating a Structured Blog Post Outline:

To begin, you'll want to direct ChatGPT to generate a detailed outline for your chosen topic. Here's an example of how to frame your prompt to guide ChatGPT in outlining a compelling and informative blog post.

Here is the corresponding prompt:

> *Create a detailed 3-paragraph outline for a blog post titled 'The ChatGPT Blueprint: Scaling Your E-commerce Business to $1 Million in Sales'.*

Using this prompt, ChatGPT will provide you with a structured outline that covers key aspects of your topic. This outline will be your guide to developing a comprehensive blog post that resonates with your audience, providing valuable insights into the strategies of successful entrepreneurs.

ChatGPT Response:

> **Blog Post Outline: "The ChatGPT Blueprint: Scaling Your E-commerce Business to $1 Million in Sales"**
>
> **Introduction**
>
> - *Start with highlighting the competitive nature of the e-commerce industry and the necessity for businesses to innovate and adopt new technologies to stand out and grow.*
> - *Introduce ChatGPT as a revolutionary AI tool that offers a wide array of applications for e-commerce businesses, from enhancing customer experience to optimizing backend operations.*
> - *The introduction will set the stage for discussing how leveraging ChatGPT can be a game-changer in scaling an e-commerce business to achieve $1 million in annual sales.*
>
> **Leveraging ChatGPT for Customer Interaction and Sales Conversion**

- *Dive into the specifics of how ChatGPT can be integrated into e-commerce platforms to personalize customer interactions, from the first point of contact through to post-purchase support.*
- *Discuss the role of ChatGPT in generating dynamic product descriptions, providing personalized recommendations, and offering 24/7 customer service.*
- *Explain how these applications not only improve the customer experience but also significantly increase conversion rates and average order values. Include success stories or case studies of e-commerce businesses that have seen tangible growth in sales and customer engagement by integrating ChatGPT into their operations.*

Implementing ChatGPT for Operational Efficiency and Market Insight

- *Shift focuses on the operational benefits of ChatGPT, detailing how it can streamline inventory management, automate responses to frequently asked questions, and assist in analyzing customer feedback for insights into market trends and preferences.*
- *Outline the process of integrating ChatGPT with existing e-commerce platforms and CRM systems to enhance efficiency, reduce overhead costs, and make data-driven decisions that align with customer needs and market opportunities.*
- *Conclude by emphasizing the strategic advantage that ChatGPT offers e-commerce businesses in scaling operations, achieving significant sales milestones, and setting a foundation for sustained growth and competitiveness in the market.*

This outline presents a concise yet comprehensive guide on harnessing ChatGPT's capabilities to drive sales and operational efficiency in e-commerce, aimed at business owners and marketers looking to achieve ambitious sales goals.

Crafting a Comprehensive Blog Post Using ChatGPT:

Having established a solid outline for your blog post, the next step is to transform this framework into a fully fleshed-out article. This methodical approach to content creation, where you first develop an outline and then expand it into a complete blog post, offers significant benefits. It allows for greater flexibility in structuring your content and ensures that the final output maintains a coherent and logical flow.

Here is the example of a prompt for expanding the blog post outline:

Expand on the provided 3-paragraph outline to create a comprehensive, in-depth blog post. Ensure the content is rich in detail and incorporates SEO principles for enhanced online visibility.

This approach not only streamlines the writing process, but also ensures that your blog post is both informative and engaging. By guiding ChatGPT through each step, from outline creation to full article development, you can craft content that not only captivates your audience but also ranks well on search engines.

ChatGPT Response:

The ChatGPT Blueprint: Scaling Your E-commerce Business to $1 Million in Sales

In the rapidly evolving landscape of e-commerce, businesses are constantly seeking innovative strategies to not only survive but thrive. The digital marketplace is fiercely competitive, with customer expectations growing by the day. In this environment, adopting cutting-edge technologies such as ChatGPT can be the differentiator that propels your e-commerce business to the coveted $1 million annual sales mark. ChatGPT, an advanced AI language model, offers a plethora of applications designed to enhance customer experiences and streamline operations, setting the stage for unprecedented growth and success.

Leveraging ChatGPT for Customer Interaction and Sales Conversion

At the heart of any successful e-commerce business is the ability to effectively engage with customers and convert these interactions into sales. ChatGPT stands out as a transformative tool in this regard. It can be seamlessly integrated into e-commerce platforms to create personalized shopping experiences that resonate with individual customers. Imagine dynamic product descriptions that adapt to user interests or instant, personalized recommendations akin to a virtual shopping assistant. ChatGPT can also power 24/7 customer service operations, handling inquiries, and providing support with a level of responsiveness and personalization that traditional customer service channels struggle to match.

(Note: I haven't included the whole blog output here as it would take up too much space. But this should give you an idea of what is possible with ChatGPT)

This content is accurate but somewhat cold, so we opted to provide an additional prompt for enhancement once the initial response was complete.

Prompt:

Please make it funnier and make the tone more friendly.

ChatGPT Response:

The ChatGPT Blueprint: Laughing Your Way to $1 Million in E-commerce Sales

Welcome to the wild, wild web of e-commerce, where the competition is tougher than a two-dollar steak and the stakes are high. But fear not, intrepid online merchant, for I bring you the secret weapon to catapult your business to the $1 million sales club - and yes, it's as exciting as finding an extra fry at the bottom of the bag. Enter stage left: ChatGPT, the AI wizard that's about to turn your e-commerce game from "meh" to "wowza"!

Turning Browsers into Buyers with a Smile

Picture this: a customer lands on your site, greeted by product descriptions so engaging they could win an Oscar. ChatGPT is your behind-the-scenes wordsmith, crafting lines that make your items irresistible - like saying your sneakers are so comfy, they feel like walking on the backs of gently sighing puppies. And customer service? Imagine a world where every query is met with responses so swift and helpful, your customers wonder if you've hired a team of mind-reading geniuses. That's the ChatGPT effect - turning every interaction into a chance to charm the socks off your clientele and keep them coming back for more, all while boosting those sales numbers.

(Note: the complete blog output is not included here due to space constraints. However, this excerpt should provide a clear understanding of ChatGPT's revised output.)

CRAFTING ENGAGING YOUTUBE/PODCAST SCRIPTS WITH CHATGPT:

Creating content for YouTube or a podcast involves significant preparation and skill, especially in crafting a script that captures and keeps audience attention. Key steps in this process include:

1. **Crafting an Engaging Introduction:** Develop an opener that immediately piques the viewer's interest.
2. **Logical Script Structure:** Organize your content coherently, using clear headings and subheadings.
3. **Accessible Language:** Ensure your script is straightforward and easy for your audience to understand.
4. **Compelling Call-to-Action:** Conclude with a persuasive call-to-action, encouraging viewers to subscribe or engage further.
5. **SEO Optimization:** Refine your script to be SEO-friendly, enhancing its online visibility.
6. **Consistency in Tone and Message:** Align your script with the overall tone and messaging of your channel.
7. **Clear and Resonant Message:** Ensure your content resonates with and applies to your target audience.

Example: Transforming a Blog into a YouTube/Podcast Script

Suppose you aim to bolster your social media presence by converting a blog post into a YouTube video or podcast episode. You can repurpose the content from your blog, adapting it into a script suitable for audio-visual media.

Example of a prompt for script creation:

Transform the blog outline titled 'Unlocking the Million-Dollar Milestone: Top Strategies Used by Successful Entrepreneurs' into a detailed, step-by-step, and engaging script suitable for a YouTube video or podcast episode.

ChatGPT Response:

[Introduction: Upbeat Music]

Host: "Hello, hello, hello! Welcome back to [Your Channel/Show Name], the place where we turn business dreams into reality! I'm your host, [Your Name], today, we're diving into something super exciting – 'Unlocking the Million-Dollar Milestone: Top Strategies Used by Successful Entrepreneurs'. So, if you've been dreaming of that seven-figure turnover, grab your notebook, and let's get into it!"

[Transition Sound Effect]

[Section 1: Understanding the Million-Dollar Mindset]

Host: "Alright, first up, let's talk about mindset. Picture this: you're on a business battlefield. The million-dollar milestone? That's your Everest. To conquer it, you need the mindset of a champion. Resilience, vision, adaptability – these aren't just buzzwords, folks, they're your armor. Remember, every setback is a setup for a comeback. So, wear that growth mindset like a superhero cape and soar!"

(Note: I haven't included the whole response here as it would take up too much space. But this should give you an idea of the quality of ChatGPT response)

NAVIGATING THE COMPLEXITIES OF SOCIAL MEDIA MARKETING:

In today's digital era, social media marketing is essential for entrepreneurs and business owners. The landscape is fiercely competitive, whether you're managing your own social media marketing or working within an agency. Here are some common challenges faced in this dynamic field:

1. **Adapting to Algorithm Changes:** Social media platforms are constantly evolving, requiring marketers to be agile and responsive to changing algorithms.
2. **Staying Ahead of Trends:** The rapid pace of innovation in social media marketing demands continuous learning to avoid falling behind.
3. **Crafting Engaging Content:** Creating content that not only engages but also aligns with your brand and resonates with your audience is crucial.
4. **Measuring ROI:** Quantifying the impact of social media campaigns on a business's bottom line is complex and often challenging.
5. **Managing Client Expectations:** Clients may have unrealistic goals or lack a deep understanding of social media marketing's nuances.
6. **Team Management:** As your agency grows, leading a team of social media professionals presents its own set of challenges.
7. **Balancing Creativity and Strategy:** It's vital to blend creative content with strategic goals to support business objectives.
8. **Budget Constraints:** Delivering impactful results while adhering to budget limitations is a key challenge.
9. **Handling Criticism:** Dealing with negative feedback is part of the job and requires resilience and professionalism.

Consider a scenario where you're heading a digital marketing agency in search of innovative content ideas for your clients. Using ChatGPT to generate high-quality content can significantly boost conversions and drive sales, benefiting both your clients and your agency.

Next, we'll explore strategies to swiftly create content across various social media channels, leveraging the capabilities of ChatGPT to streamline the process and enhance content quality.

Example: Developing a Comprehensive Marketing Campaign

Imagine you're tasked with presenting an on-the-spot advertising campaign proposal to a client launching their career as a Beauty and Fitness Coach. They require a detailed overview of the campaign's structure and strategy.

To effectively tackle this task, employing the "Act as" prompt with ChatGPT can be incredibly beneficial. This approach allows you to simulate the expertise of an advertising agency executive, enabling the creation of a well-rounded marketing campaign.

Here is the prompt:

> *Act as a seasoned advertising agency executive. Develop a thorough and targeted marketing campaign for a new Beauty and Fitness Coach. This campaign should identify the ideal target audience, craft compelling key messages and slogans, select appropriate media channels for promotion, and outline any supplementary activities necessary to achieve the desired outreach and impact for developing brand awareness.*

This prompt guides ChatGPT to construct a marketing strategy that encompasses all essential elements, from audience targeting to media planning. It's a comprehensive approach that ensures every aspect of the campaign aligns with the client's objectives and the specific nuances of the Beauty and Fitness industry. In the preceding prompt, substitute *"Beauty and Fitness Coach"* with the specific product or service you aim to highlight on social media platforms.

ChatGPT Response:

> **Campaign Title: "Empower Your Beauty and Fitness Journey with [Coach's Name]"**
>
> **1. Target Audience Identification:**
>
> **Primary Audience**: *Women aged 25-45, health-conscious, interested in fitness and beauty, likely to be active on social media, and looking for holistic wellness solutions.*
>
> **Secondary Audience**: *Men and women aged 20-30, fitness enthusiasts, and those beginning their wellness journey, interested in personalized coaching and lifestyle improvement.*
>
> **2. Key Messages and Slogans:**
>
> **Main Message**: *"Transform Your Life, Inside and Out."*

Slogans:

- *"Beauty in Strength, Strength in Beauty."*
- *"Your Personalized Path to Wellness Awaits."*
- *"Fitness Meets Beauty – Empowered, Enhanced, You."*

3. Media Channels for Promotion:

Social Media:

Instagram and Facebook for daily posts and stories showcasing Client transformations, workout tips, beauty routines, and motivational content. YouTube for longer form content, including workout routines, beauty tutorials, and client testimonials.

Influencer Partnerships: *Collaborate with micro-influencers in the beauty and fitness niche to tap into established follower bases.*

Content Marketing: *A dedicated blog on the coach's website featuring articles on fitness tips, beauty advice, nutrition, and wellness. Guest blogging on popular health and wellness websites.*

(Note: I've provided only the first part of the output from ChatGPT. This gives you a glimpse into what ChatGPT could do for your business or projects).

Example: Crafting an Instagram Post for a Sustainable Beauty Subscription Box

Envision your client is introducing a unique subscription box service, focusing on eco-friendly and sustainable beauty products. Each month, subscribers receive a carefully curated selection of items, including skincare, haircare, makeup, and wellness products.

To effectively promote this service on Instagram, you can leverage ChatGPT's capabilities to emulate a skilled marketing agency copywriter with expertise in the beauty industry. Here's how you can frame your prompt:

Act as a seasoned marketing agency copywriter with a deep understanding of the beauty industry. Craft a captivating Instagram post to promote the new eco-friendly and sustainable beauty subscription box service. Highlight the unique aspects of the service, including its monthly curation of skincare, haircare, makeup, and wellness products.

ChatGPT Response:

Unveiling Nature's Magic in a Box!

Hey, eco-beauty enthusiasts! Get ready to immerse yourself in a world where sustainability meets luxury. Introducing our all-new Eco-Friendly Beauty Subscription Box – your monthly rendezvous with the best of nature's o'ferings! Each box is a treasure trove of handpicked delights, carefully curated to pamper you from head to toe.

Imagine unboxing a surprise every month, filled with the purest skincare, nourishing haircare, vibrant makeup, and holistic wellness products. 🌿 💄

What makes our box stand out?
📦 *Cruelty-Free Goodness: We say NO to animal testing. Only the kindest, love-filled products here!*
🌿 *Plant-Powered Ingredients: Sourced from Mother Earth, harnessing her natural healing and beautifying powers.*
🍃 *Sustainable Packaging: We're not only about what is inside the box; we care about the planet too. Our packaging is as green as our mission.*
Top-Quality Selection: Each product is chosen for its effectiveness, safety, and ethical production.

Ready to embark on a guilt-free beauty journey?
💚 *Subscribe now and be part of the movement that is challenging the face of beauty – one eco-friendly box at a time!*

#EcoBeautyBox #SustainableGlam #GreenBeautyJourney #BeautyWithAPurpose #UnboxHappiness

[Image suggestion: A beautifully arranged selection of natural beauty products in an open, recyclable box, surrounded by green leaves and flowers, conveying an eco-friendly and luxurious feel.]

Streamlining Social Media Content Creation Across Platforms:

In today's digital landscape, a company's presence across multiple social media platforms is essential. Creating tailored content for each platform, especially for Twitter (currently known as X) with its unique format and character limits, traditionally demands starting anew for each post.

However, ChatGPT significantly simplifies this challenge. You can effortlessly adapt content to suit different social media platforms, including Twitter, with just a simple prompt. Here's an example of how to transform existing content into an engaging tweet:

Example: Adapting Content for Twitter

Prompt:

Act as marketing expert, transform the provided content into a captivating tweet, ensuring it is concise yet impactful for Twitter's format.

ChatGPT Response:

✍ ✍ Discover the magic of sustainability with our Eco-Friendly Beauty Subscription Box! ✍ Each month, indulge in cruelty-free skincare, haircare, makeup, and wellness, all wrapped in green packaging. Join the #EcoBeauty revolution! 💚 #SustainableGlam #UnboxHappiness ✨🎁

When adapting a post for Twitter, the content must be succinct yet engaging because of the platform's character limit. ChatGPT skillfully condenses the core message, emphasizing the primary appeal of the subscription box and its eco-friendly nature. It incorporates a clear call-to-action and relevant hashtags to boost the post's outreach. Including emojis adds an appealing touch, fostering a sense of connection with an audience keen on sustainable living.

Maximizing Efficiency with Cross-Platform Content Adaptation:

Continuing this strategy, you can effortlessly repurpose your initial post for platforms like Facebook, LinkedIn, Pinterest, or even script a TikTok video. This method not only saves time but also ensures uniformity in tone and branding across different channels with minimal effort.

Consider an example where you're operating an e-commerce store specializing in digital wall art products. Using ChatGPT to craft compelling product descriptions for platforms like Etsy or your online store can significantly pique interest and boost sales. ChatGPT can help to create effective email marketing campaigns. These campaigns can highlight your products while offering special discounts or promotions to your subscriber base.

Generating engaging, shareable content for platforms like Pinterest, Twitter, and Instagram is much more manageable. This broader reach can help you build a dedicated following. Capitalizing on trending topics and hashtags can further enhance your content's impact, potentially leading to viral exposure and a significant increase in traffic and brand visibility.

Example: Crafting an Etsy Product Description for Digital Art

Prompt:

Compose a product listing for a digital art piece in a vintage style, suitable for an Etsy storefront.

ChatGPT Response:

Timeless Elegance: Vintage-Style Digital Art Print

Step back in time with "Timeless Elegance," a stunning digital art piece that captures the essence of vintage charm. Perfect for lovers of classic style and nostalgic beauty, this print adds a touch of bygone elegance to any space.

Features:

- **Handcrafted Digital Art**: Each piece is digitally crafted with attention to detail, ensuring a unique vintage appeal.
- **High-Quality Print**: Printed on premium, archival-grade paper for a fade-resistant finish that lasts.
- **Size Options**: Available in multiple sizes to fit your space perfectly (8x10, 11x14, 16x20 inches).
- **Customizable**: Option to customize colors to match your decor at no extra cost.
- **Instant Classic**: A timeless addition to your home, office, or as a thoughtful gift.
- **Easy to Frame**: Delivered unframed, ready for you to frame in the style that best suits your interior.
- **Secure Packaging**: Shipped in a sturdy, protective tube to ensure it arrives in pristine condition.

How It's Made: "Timeless Elegance" is born from a blend of modern digital Artistry and vintage inspiration. Using advanced digital techniques, the artist creates a piece that echoes the textures and tones of traditional art, while the subject matter pays homage to the classic era.

Usage Ideas:

- Elevate your living room or bedroom decor with a touch of vintage elegance.
- Enhance your office or study with this sophisticated art piece.
- A perfect gift for art lovers, vintage enthusiasts, or anyone who appreciates timeless beauty.

Example: Crafting LinkedIn Posts for Personal Branding

Suppose you're building a personal brand in professional coaching and aim to expand your LinkedIn following by sharing valuable insights.

Prompt:

> Craft a LinkedIn post in a compelling tone that emphasizes the significance of professional coaching for entrepreneurs.

ChatGPT Response:

> 🚀 **Unlock Your Entrepreneurial Potential: The Power of Professional Coaching** 🚀
>
> Hello LinkedIn community! Today, I want to spotlight a game-changer in the entrepreneurial journey – Professional Coaching.
>
> As entrepreneurs, we often find ourselves in uncharted waters, navigating the complex world of business. It's an'exhi'arating ride, but let's be'hone't, it can also be daunting.

That's wh're p'ofessional coaching steps in as a lighthouse, guiding us through the fog of uncertainty.

🔍 *Why Professional Coaching?*

__Clarity in Vision__: Coaches help crystalize your goals, turning vague ideas into actionable plans.

__Strategic Insight__: Benefit from their wealth of experience, avoiding common pitfalls and accelerating growth.

__Accountability__: A coach keeps you on track, turning procrastination into productivity.

__Personal Growth__: It's not just about business growth; it's about evolving as a leader and a person.

✒ __Impact on Entrepreneurs__: From my experience, entrepreneurs who embrace coaching see remarkable transformations. They achieve their goals faster, make smarter decisions, and develop resilience to face business challenges. It's not an expense; it's an investment in your biggest asset - YOU!

🌐 __In a World of Constant Change__: In today's fast-paced business environment, staying ahead is key. A professional coach equips you with the tools to adapt, innovate, and lead with confidence.

So, I encourage my fellow entrepreneurs: consider professional coaching. It could be the catalyst that propels your business – and your personal development – to new heights.

Have you had a positive experience with professional coaching? Share your stories in the comments. Let's inspire and learn from each other!

#Entrepreneurship #ProfessionalCoaching #BusinessGrowth #LeadershipDevelopment #Innovation

BUSINESS SERVICES FOR CUSTOMIZED DIET AND EXERCISE PLANS:

Imagine running a business that offers personalized diet and exercise plans, catering to clients who lack the time for extensive research or the resources to hire a dietician or personal trainer. This service eliminates the need for clients to delve deep into complex nutritional topics like carbohydrates, keto diets, macros, or caloric deficits (however, make sure you have the background and licenses to touch on this type of topics). Similarly, for exercise routines, clients won't have time to spend hours learning about muscle groups and exercise routines.

In this scenario, ChatGPT becomes an invaluable tool. Not only can it develop customized diet plans, but it also aligns exercise regimes with these dietary guidelines, offering a holistic approach to health and fitness. This service is especially beneficial for professionals in the health and wellness industry, such as personal trainers, nutritionists, and dieticians, saving them significant time in client plan development.

Example: Creating Personalized Health Plans

Let's demonstrate how ChatGPT can craft custom diet and exercise plans that consider all aspects of an individual's health profile, preferences, and goals. This approach ensures clients receive a comprehensive, tailored plan that aligns with their unique needs and lifestyle, enhancing the effectiveness of your service offerings.

Prompt:

Assume the role of a dietician and develop a comprehensive 2-week diet plan tailored for a 35-year-old vegetarian male, who is 6 feet tall and weighs 220 pounds, aiming to lose a pound per week. The diet should provide a detailed caloric breakdown and adhere to a macro distribution of 50% carbohydrates, 15% fats, and 35% protein.

ChatGPT Response:

Creating a comprehensive 2-week diet plan for a 35-year-old vegetarian male aiming to lose weight requires careful consideration of nutritional needs and caloric intake. For weight loss of about a pound per week, a moderate caloric deficit is recommended.

Given the individual's height, weight, and physical activity level (not specified but assumed to be moderate), his daily caloric needs for weight maintenance are roughly estimated to be around 2800 calories.

To lose weight at a healthy rate, reducing daily intake by about 500 calories is a good target, leading to an intake of approximately 2300 calories per day.

The requested macro distribution is 50% carbohydrates, 35% protein, and 15% fats. Here's a detailed plan:

Day 1-7:

Breakfast: Oatmeal with Almond Milk and Berries
- *Calories: ~400*
- *Macros: Carbs 60g, Protein 20g, Fats 7g*

Mid-Morning Snack: Greek Yogurt with Nuts
- *Calories: ~300*
- *Macros: Carbs 25g, Protein 20g, Fats 10g*

Lunch: Quinoa and Black Bean Salad with Avocado
- *Calories: ~600*
- *Macros: Carbs 70g, Protein 30g, Fats 20g*

Afternoon Snack: Hummus and Carrot Sticks
- *Calories: ~200*
- *Macros: Carbs 25g, Protein 10g, Fats 8g*

(Note: Here's just the beginning of what ChatGPT offered. It showcases the depth of detail you can expect.)

Example: Integrating Diet and Exercise for a Customized Workout Plan

To create a truly personalized experience for your client, ChatGPT can use the previously outlined dietary context to develop a workout plan that not only suits the client's physical characteristics and goals but also complements his nutritional regimen.

Prompt:

Considering the specified vegetarian diet plan, devise an exercise routine for the same client that aligns with both his dietary habits and fitness objectives.

ChatGPT Response:

For the 35-year-old vegetarian male, aiming to lose weight while maintaining muscle mass, a well-rounded exercise routine that balances cardiovascular workouts with strength training is ideal. Given his goal of losing a pound a week and his vegetarian diet, the exercise routine should complement his dietary intake to ensure he gets enough energy and nutrients to support his workout regimen.

Weekly Exercise Plan:

Day 1: Strength Training - Upper Body

- *Warm-up: 10 minutes brisk walking or jogging*
- *Circuit (Repeat 3 times):*
- *Bench Press or Push-ups: 3 sets of 10-12 reps*
- *Dumbbell Rows or Bodyweight Rows: 3 sets of 10-12 reps*
- *Shoulder Press: 3 sets of 10-12 reps*
- *Bicep Curls: 3 sets of 10-12 reps*
- *Tricep Dips: 3 sets of 10-12 reps*
- *Cool Down: Stretching – 10 minutes*

(Note: Please find the initial segment of ChatGPT's output above. This excerpt is intended to demonstrate the comprehensive level of detail provided by ChatGPT.)

OPTIMIZING ONLINE EDUCATION WITH CUSTOMIZED LEARNING PLANS:

Navigating the challenges of online education requires balancing several tasks: staying competitive, interacting with customers, grading assignments, and crafting exams. Determining the difficulty level for your content while ensuring it can be completed within a reasonable timeframe is one of the most daunting tasks. This process is not only time intensive but also requires a keen understanding of educational needs and student capabilities.

This scenario is common whether you're a schoolteacher, a private tutor, or an online course creator. The good news is that tools like ChatGPT significantly reduce the burden of creating lesson plans and course ideas.

Example: Creating Course Concepts for Online Platforms

Let's explore how ChatGPT can help generate ideas for online courses, especially if your expertise lies in makeup and beauty, and you're targeting a professional audience on platforms like LinkedIn Learning.

Prompt:

> *Generate a list of 5 innovative online course ideas that I can offer on LinkedIn Learning, tailored to my expertise in makeup and beauty, and catering to the professional audience on LinkedIn.*

ChatGPT Response:

> **Strategic Branding for Beauty Entrepreneurs**: *This course would focus on developing a strong personal and business brand in the beauty industry. It will cover topics like identifying your unique value proposition, effective brand communication, and leveraging digital platforms to build a loyal customer base.*
>
> **Digital Transformation in the Beauty Industry**: *Aimed at beauty professionals and business owners, this course would explore how to integrate digital tools and technologies into traditional beauty practices, including online consultations, virtual try-on apps, and digital marketing strategies.*
>
> **Professional Makeup Techniques for Video Conferencing**: *Tailored for the remote work era, this course would teach makeup applications that are camera-friendly for video calls, addressing issues like lighting, color correction, and makeup that translates well on-screen.*
>
> **Sustainable Practices in Beauty Care**: *This course would offer insights into incorporating sustainable and eco-friendly practices in beauty routines and businesses. Topics would include selecting sustainable products, minimizing waste, and advocating for green practices in the beauty industry.*
>
> **Advanced Skincare Science for Beauty Professionals**: *Designed for beauty experts, this course would delve into the science behind skincare. It would cover understanding different skin types, the science of skincare ingredients, and how to personalize skincare routines for clients based on scientific principles.*
>
> *These course ideas are designed to provide value to professionals in the makeup and beauty industry on LinkedIn Learning, offering advanced knowledge and skills relevant to current trends and industry needs.*

OPTIMIZING PRODUCTIVITY FOR INCOME GENERATION WITH CHATGPT:

To enhance productivity and boost income through current endeavors or new business ideas using ChatGPT, you can adopt the following strategies. Please note that you can implement the strategies outlined below using the specific GPT models provided in this book.

1. **Idea Generation and Validation**: Utilize ChatGPT to brainstorm innovative business ideas or explore ways to expand current ventures. It can help validate these ideas by analyzing market trends, potential competition, and customer demand.
2. **Efficient Task Management**: Employ ChatGPT to streamline routine tasks such as email communication, scheduling, and basic research. This frees up time to focus on strategic and creative aspects of your business.
3. **Enhancing Content Creation**: For content creators, ChatGPT can be a valuable tool in generating initial drafts, blog topics, social media posts, or even script ideas. It helps maintain a consistent content flow, crucial for audience engagement and monetization.
4. **Market Research and Analysis**: Use ChatGPT to conduct preliminary market research. It can gather data on market trends, customer preferences, and industry benchmarks, aiding in informed decision-making.
5. **Skill Development and Learning**: ChatGPT can be a learning assistant, providing explanations, resources, and tutorials on various topics, helping you gain new skills or enhance existing ones crucial for business growth.
6. **Automation of Repetitive Tasks**: Automate repetitive business tasks using ChatGPT. For instance, generating standardized responses to common customer inquiries or automating parts of your content creation process.
7. **Networking and Outreach**: ChatGPT can help draft personalized outreach messages for networking, partnership opportunities, or client acquisition, helping to expand your professional network and business opportunities.
8. **Productivity Tips and Strategies**: Ask ChatGPT for productivity tips and time management strategies tailored to your specific business context, helping to optimize your daily routines and work efficiency.
9. **Customized Solutions for Business Challenges**: Present your business challenges to ChatGPT for creative solutions and strategies. It can offer diverse perspectives and solutions you might not have considered.
10. **Evaluation and Improvement of Business Processes**: Use ChatGPT to evaluate and suggest improvements for your business processes, ensuring they are efficient and aligned with your business goals.

By leveraging the capabilities of ChatGPT in these areas, you can significantly enhance your productivity, leading to increased income generation from your current business activities or new entrepreneurial ventures.

Chapter 15
LEVERAGING CHATGPT FOR SUSTAINABLE PASSIVE INCOME OPPORTUNITIES

The landscape for generating passive income has evolved dramatically. With ChatGPT, opportunities with low entry barriers are becoming increasingly saturated. This shift requires a strategic approach to identify and develop income streams that are not easily replicated.

To stay ahead of the curve, we'll concentrate on avenues that, even with the aid of ChatGPT, demand effort and creativity to excel. These are areas where high-quality, unique content is key and where a single prompt to ChatGPT won't be enough to create something of value. By focusing on these niches, you can ensure your content stands out in a market less likely to be overwhelmed by mass-produced offerings.

Our focus will be on the following areas:

    A. Books
    B. Youtube Videos
    C. Blog Posts
    D. Online Courses
    E. Digital Wall Art
    F. Print-on-Demand Clothing

A. BOOKS

Books (whether e-books or physical books) represent a significant opportunity for generating passive income. While crafting a successful book demands considerable initial effort, the potential for long-term royalties is substantial.

Platforms like Amazon's Kindle Direct Publishing (KDP) and Ingram Spark offer comprehensive services for self-publishers, including print-on-demand (POD) for physical books and distribution for both physical and electronic books. These platforms enable authors to publish and distribute their books globally without the need to maintain a physical inventory, facilitating access to a wide network of retailers based on their reach and agreements. Other platforms include Apple Books, Barnes & Noble, and Kobo.

Creating a compelling book involves several key steps:

1. Identifying an engaging and profitable topic and niche.
2. Conducting in-depth research to ensure the content is credible and comprehensive.
3. Structuring the material coherently and logically for easy comprehension.
4. Writing content that captivates and keeps the reader's interest throughout.
5. Adapting your writing style to resonate with your intended audience and ensuring readability.
6. Formatting the book to be visually appealing and functional across various readers.
7. Meticulously proofreading and editing to eliminate errors and enhance clarity.
8. Designing an eye-catching cover that differentiates your book in a crowded market.
9. Implementing effective marketing strategies to promote the book to its target audience.
10. Strategically pricing the book to optimize sales, considering your market and audience.

Fortunately, ChatGPT can assist significantly in many of these areas. Let's begin with the crucial first step: identifying a profitable niche.

Example: Identifying Your Book Niche and Topic

If you're uncertain about which niche to choose for your book, a brainstorming session using ChatGPT can be incredibly helpful. To further enhance this exercise, we recommend thoroughly reviewing the platform you want to use, ensuring a comprehensive approach to selecting the most suitable niche for your work.

Prompt:

Act as an Amazon KDP publisher expert. List 5 unique and potentially profitable niches suitable for writing an ebook.

ChatGPT Response:

As an Amazon KDP publisher expert, identifying unique and potentially profitable niches is crucial for standing out in a saturated market. Here are some niche ideas suitable for writing a book:

Green Profits Eco-Entrepreneurship as a Side Hustle*: With growing awareness of environmental issues, this book focuses on how to start a side hustle in the green economy.*

Plant-Based Nutrition for Athletes*: Cater to the growing number of athletes looking for vegan and vegetarian nutrition guides to enhance performance.*

Mindful Technology Use*: Addressing the balance between connectivity and digital detox in a tech-saturated society.*

Heritage Cooking Techniques*: Dive into traditional cooking methods from various cultures that are at risk of being forgotten.*

Urban Homesteading*: Guide city dwellers on how to grow food, raise small livestock, and adopt sustainable living practices in limited spaces.*

By focusing on these niches, you can cater to specific audiences looking for expert knowledge, which can translate into profitable book opportunities on Amazon KDP.

To narrow down your book topic within a specific niche, such as 'Green Profits: Eco-Entrepreneurship as a Side Hustle', you can use ChatGPT to generate more targeted ideas.

Prompt:

Provide 5 specific topics I can explore within the niche of 'Green Profits: Eco-Entrepreneurship as a Side Hustle'.

ChatGPT Response:

Zero-Waste Startups: Crafting a Business Model that Embraces Sustainability
- *Dive into the principles of zero-waste and how to build a business plan that prioritizes sustainability.*
- *Cover case studies of successful zero-waste businesses, from packaging-free stores to upcycled goods.*

Eco-Friendly Apparel: Capitalizing on the Sustainable Fashion Movement

- *Explore the burgeoning market for sustainable clothing and accessories. Discuss how to source eco-friendly materials, the logistics of sustainable manufacturing, and marketing strategies for reaching environmentally conscious consumers.*

Organic Urban Gardening: Growing Profits through Local Produce

- *Offer insights on starting an organic garden in urban settings and turning it into a profitable venture. Discuss vertical farming, community-supported agriculture (CSA), and strategies for local distribution and marketing.*

Renewable Energy Solutions for Home and Business

- *Discuss the potential for side hustles in the renewable energy sector, such as becoming a solar panel distributor or starting a consultancy for businesses looking to reduce their carbon footprint.*

Sustainable Event Planning: Creating Eco-Friendly Experiences

- *Delve into the niche of green event planning. Cover topics such as sourcing sustainable venues, waste reduction methods, eco-friendly catering, and marketing eco-events to a target audience.*

Each of these topics not only provides a viable business idea but also aligns with the growing consumer demand for sustainable and ethical practices, which is key for eco-entrepreneurship.

Example: Crafting a Book Outline

Once you've chosen a topic for your book, such as 'Eco-Friendly Apparel: Capitalizing on the Sustainable Fashion Movement,' the next step is to develop a comprehensive outline. This will serve as the framework for your book.

Prompt:

Generate a detailed outline for the book titled 'Eco-Friendly Apparel: Capitalizing on the Sustainable Fashion Movement'.

ChatGPT Response:

Title: "Eco-Friendly Apparel: Capitalizing on the Sustainable Fashion Movement"

Introduction:

- *Explain the rise of the sustainable fashion movement.*
- *Outline the environmental and ethical motivations behind eco-friendly apparel.*
- *Present the book's objectives: educating aspiring entrepreneurs about launching a sustainable fashion brand, navigating the market, and making a positive impact.*

Chapter 1: The Green Wardrobe Revolution

- *History of fashion and its environmental impact.*
- *The awakening of consumer consciousness towards eco-friendly apparel.*
- *Case studies of successful sustainable fashion brands.*

Chapter 2: Understanding Sustainable Fashion

- *Definition and principles of sustainable fashion.*
- *Differentiating between greenwashing and genuine practices.*
- *The lifecycle of sustainable clothing from raw materials to disposal.*

Chapter 3: Sourcing Materials

- *Identifying and sourcing eco-friendly fabrics and materials.*
- *Building relationships with ethical suppliers.*
- *Certifications and standards to look for in sustainable materials.*

(Note: Please find the initial segment of ChatGPT's output above. This excerpt should demonstrate the comprehensive level of detail provided by the AI.)

Keep in mind that the provided outline is merely a starting point. Based on your research and the interests of your target audience, you might find it necessary to change the structure. Add or omit topics to better align with your vision. Additionally, consider expanding each section with more subtopics to thoroughly cover every aspect of your chosen subject.

Example: Developing Chapter Outlines

With your book outline as a guide, you can delve deeper into creating detailed outlines for each chapter.

Prompt:

Develop a detailed chapter outline for 'Chapter I: The Green Wardrobe Revolution'.

ChatGPT Response:

Chapter I: The Green Wardrobe Revolution

Introduction to the Chapter:

- *Brief overview of the fashion industry's evolution.*
- *Introduction to the concept of the 'Green Wardrobe'.*
- *Significance of the revolution in contemporary fashion.*

Section 1: The Fabric of History

- *A brief history of fashion from industrialization to present day.*
- *The rise of 'fast fashion' and its global footprint.*

- *Pioneering moments that sparked the sustainable fashion conversation.*

Section 2: Environmental Wake-Up Call

- *Statistics and facts on the environmental impact of the fashion industry.*
- *Case studies of environmental degradation caused by fashion production.*
- *The role of consumer awareness in catalyzing change.*

Section 3: Ethical Fashion: More Than a Trend

- *Definition and pillars of ethical fashion.*
- *Ethical considerations in fashion, from labor rights to animal welfare.*
- *Profiles of activists and movements advocating for ethical fashion.*

(Note: Above is a segment from ChatGPT response, showcasing the depth and thoroughness of the AI-generated content.)

Developing Comprehensive Chapter Content:

Once you've crafted individual chapter outlines for your book, as showed above, you're well on your way to constructing the complete structure for each chapter. Utilizing these detailed outlines, you can seamlessly progress to creating the actual content for each chapter.

Example: Writing Chapter Introduction

To illustrate, let's develop the introductory content for a chapter.

Prompt:

Based on the provided outline for 'Chapter I: The Green Wardrobe Revolution', compose a 250-word introduction to this chapter.

ChatGPT Response:

Welcome to the dawn of a transformative era in fashion—an era where the threads that weave our garments together tell a story far beyond style and trend, a narrative of ecological awareness and ethical responsibility. 'The Green Wardrobe Revolution' is not just a chapter in this book; it's an unfolding chapter in the world's history, marking a pivotal shift from the once-unquestioned norms of the fashion industry to a new paradigm that champions sustainability.

Once, the rhythm of fashion beat to the seasonal cycles of spring/summer and fall/winter collections, but the relentless pace of 'fast fashion' has accelerated this cycle, leading to environmental strain and ethical quandaries. As the consequences of this relentless pace have become starkly visible, a revolution has begun. Not with the clashing of swords, but with the clipping of scissors, the stitching of eco-friendly fabrics, and the choices of conscious consumers.

In this chapter, we will unravel the threads of the past to understand how the fabric of fashion has been dyed in the hues of industrialization and modernization, only to find a burgeoning need for change. We will explore the environmental wake-up calls that jolted the world into action and the ethical imperatives that fashion as a force for good can no longer ignore.

Through a tapestry of pioneering moments, influential movements, and case studies of trailblazing brands, we will illustrate the emergence and impact of the sustainable fashion movement. This chapter is a tribute to the revolution that is dressing the world in hope, responsibility, and green innovation—one garment at a time. Welcome to the Green Wardrobe Revolution.

Example: Brainstorming Book Titles and Subtitles

Next, let's focus on generating a creative and compelling title and subtitle for your book, capturing the essence of its theme.

Prompt:

Act as a marketing copywriter. Provide several engaging book titles and subtitles suitable for this eco-entrepreneurship themed book. This is important for the success of my book.

ChatGPT Response:

1. Title: "Verde Vogue: Dressing the Future in Sustainability"
   Subtitle: "A Revolutionary Guide to Eco-Entrepreneurship in the Fashion Industry"

2. Title: "Eco Ensemble: The Art of Sustainable Style"
   Subtitle: "Transforming Passion for Fashion into Environmental Action"

3. Title: "Sustainable Stitches: Crafting a Greener Fashion Legacy"
   Subtitle: "The Entrepreneur's Guide to Eco-Friendly Apparel Innovation"

4. Title: "Green Garments: Sewing the Seeds of Change in Fashion"
   Subtitle: "How to Weave Eco-Principles into a Profitable Brand Narrative"

5. Title: "The Conscious Closet Creator: Tailoring a Million-Dollar Eco Brand"
   Subtitle: "Strategies for Success in the Sustainable Fashion Revolution"

Each of these titles combines a sense of eco-consciousness with the allure of the fashion industry, aimed at engaging potential readers who are passionate about making a difference while building a profitable business.

Example: Crafting a Sales Page Book Description

Having established the context and content of your book within ChatGPT, you can effortlessly instruct it to create a compelling book description. You can use this for your

Amazon product listing or any other online sales platform.

Prompt:

> Please create a descriptive and engaging sales page for the book with the title 'Verde Vogue: Dressing the Future in Sustainability' and subtitle 'A Revolutionary Guide to Eco-Entrepreneurship in the Fashion Industry'

ChatGPT Response:

Unveil the Green in Fashion with "Verde Vogue" - Where Style Meets Sustainability Welcome to a movement where the tapestry of fashion is interwoven with the vibrant hues of eco-consciousness. "Verde Vogue: Dressing the Future in Sustainability" isn't just a book; it's a manifesto for a revolution, a call to action for innovators and dreamers who envision a world where fashion thrives in harmony with our planet.

About the Book: *In the pages of "Verde Vogue," you'll embark on a journey through the heart of the sustainable fashion movement. This is more than a guide; it's an exploration into the soul of eco-friendly design, a map that leads you through the rich landscape of ethical entrepreneurship in the fashion industry.*

Features:

- ***Insightful Forewords*** *by renowned eco-fashion pioneers.*
- ***In-Depth Analysis*** *of the environmental impact of the fashion industry.*
- ***Exclusive Interviews*** *with leading sustainable fashion brand owners.*
- ***Practical Steps*** *to build your eco-friendly fashion brand from the ground up.*
- ***Comprehensive Resources*** *for sustainable materials and ethical manufacturing.*

Who Is This Book For?

- ***Aspiring Entrepreneurs*** *who dream of launching a fashion brand that*
- *aligns with their values.*
- ***Established Designers*** *looking to pivot towards more sustainable practices.*
- ***Fashion Students*** *who want to be at the forefront of the eco-fashion wave.*
- ***Conscious Consumers*** *seeking to understand the industry's shift to green.*

What You'll Learn:

- *How to **source sustainable materials** that don't compromise on quality.*
- *Strategies to **market your eco-brand** effectively in a competitive industry.*
- *The secrets to **crafting a brand story** that resonates with*
- *eco-conscious consumers.*
- *Ways to **navigate the challenges** of the sustainable fashion landscape*
- *with grace and resilience.*

Special Section: *"The Green Blueprint" - Your actionable plan for launching an eco-*

friendly line, complete with checklists, timelines, and budget guides.

Bonuses:

- **Access to an exclusive online community** *of eco-fashion entrepreneurs.*
- **Worksheets and templates** *to help refine your business plan.*
- **Free webinar** *on sustainable fashion trends with industry experts.*

Remember, the suggested product listing is just one approach. You have the flexibility to change it to better suit your book's unique focus, cater to your target audience, and reflect your preferred writing style.

Example: Crafting a Book Marketing Email

One of the significant advantages of using ChatGPT is its ability to generate a marketing email for your book seamlessly, without requiring additional input. This feature streamlines the process, making your marketing efforts more efficient.

Prompt:

Create a marketing email for the book with the title 'Verde Vogue: Dressing the Future in Sustainability' and subtitle 'A Revolutionary Guide to Eco-Entrepreneurship in the Fashion Industry'

ChatGPT Response:

Subject: Step Into the Future of Fashion with "Verde Vogue"

Dear Fashion Innovator,

Are you ready to be at the forefront of a revolution? To merge your passion for fashion with a commitment to sustainability? We are thrilled to introduce you to a game-changing new book, "Verde Vogue: Dressing the Future in Sustainability"– a revolutionary guide that is reshaping the landscape of eco-entrepreneurship in the fashion industry.

Why "Verde Vogue" In an era where the fashion industry faces critical scrutiny for its environmental impact, "Verde Vogue" emerges as a beacon of hope and action. Authored by leading voices in sustainable fashion, this book is more than a guide – it is a journey into the heart of eco-conscious apparel creation.

What is Inside?

- *Inspirational Stories: Learn from pioneers who have successfully navigated the path of sustainable fashion.*
- *Practical Tools: From sourcing eco-friendly materials to marketing your brand, get hands-on tools that make a difference.*

- **_Innovative Strategies_**: _Discover how to create not just a brand, but a movement that resonates with today's conscious consumers._

Exclusive Offer for Our Subscribers _Pre-order "Verde Vogue" now and get an exclusive 20% discount! Plus, gain early access to our online masterclass, sustainable Fashion 101 hosted by industry experts._

Be the Change _This isn't just about making fashion. It's about making a difference. "Verde Vogue" is your first step towards creating a brand that not only looks good but also does good._

Don't miss this opportunity to be a part of the sustainable fashion revolution. Pre-order your copy of "Verde Vogue" today and embrace the change.

Embrace Style, Sustainably, [Your Name] [Your Position] [Your Company]

P.S. Stay tuned for our upcoming webinar featuring "Verde Vogue" authors sharing insights on eco-friendly trends in fashion. Reserve your spot now!

You have the flexibility to modify the email content to align with your unique voice and audience. Be sure to incorporate a compelling call-to-action and provide simple instructions on how to purchase your book.

Example: Crafting a Twitter Announcement

Similarly, you can effortlessly instruct ChatGPT to create a succinct and engaging Twitter announcement for your book.

Prompt:

Create a Twitter announcement for the release of the book with the title '_Verde Vogue: Dressing the Future in Sustainability_' and subtitle '_A Revolutionary Guide to Eco-Entrepreneurship in the Fashion Industry_'.

ChatGPT Response:

Exciting News! _"Verde Vogue: Dressing the Future in Sustainability" is now available!_ _Dive into the heart of eco-entrepreneurship in fashion and be part of a stylish revolution that cares for our planet._ 🌍 _#VerdeVogue #SustainableFashion #EcoEntrepreneurship #FashionRevolution_ 📖 _Get your copy: [Link to Book]_ 📖

Example: Conducting Pricing Research

ChatGPT can help determine an optimal pricing strategy for your book based on your target market and the specific marketplace dynamics. This can help in maximizing sales potential.

Prompt:

For listing this book on Amazon, could you suggest a pricing strategy that would effectively maximize sales, considering my target audience?

ChatGPT Response:

When pricing your book "Verde Vogue: Dressing the Future in Sustainability" on Amazon, it's essential to consider several key factors that can influence sales, including your target audience, the competitive landscape, production costs, and the perceived value of your content. Here's a strategy to maximize sales effectively:

Research Competitor Pricing*: Start by analyzing the prices of similar books in the eco-entrepreneurship and sustainable fashion niche. This will give you an idea of the current market rate and help you position your book competitively.*

Introductory Offer*: Initially, set a lower introductory price to attract early buyers and generate buzz. For example, if competitive books are priced around $9.99, you might start at $6.99 or $7.99. This strategy can also help garner initial reviews, which are crucial for long-term success on Amazon.*

Assess Your Target Audience*: Consider the purchasing power and spending habits of your target audience. Professionals and entrepreneurs in the fashion industry may be willing to pay a premium for valuable insights and guidance, but the price still needs to be within a reasonable range.*

Utilize Amazon's KDP Select*: Enrolling your book in Amazon KDP Select for a 90-day period gives you promotional benefits like the Kindle Countdown Deal or Free Book Promotion. These promotions can boost visibility and drive up sales, after which you can adjust the price based on the response.*

Consider a Tiered Pricing Strategy*: After the initial launch period, you can gradually increase the price. Monitor sales and reviews closely; if they remain steady or improve with the price increase, you've found a sweet spot.*

Bundle with Other Products*: If you have other books or courses, consider bundling them with your new book at a discounted rate. This can provide more value to your customers and increase overall sales.*

Regularly Review and Adjust*: The book market can be dynamic. Regularly review your sales data, customer feedback, and market trends to adjust your pricing strategy accordingly.*

Leverage Amazon Analytics*: Use Amazon's detailed sales analytics to understand how price changes impact your sales and optimize accordingly.*

By starting with a competitive, introductory price and then adjusting based on market response and analytics, you can effectively maximize sales while maintaining the

Leveraging ChatGPT for Book Creation and Marketing:

Creating and marketing a book using ChatGPT involves several strategic steps. Here is a step-by-step guide to maximizing your use of ChatGPT for these objectives:

1. **Niche Identification**: Use ChatGPT to brainstorm and identify unique niches and topics that resonate with your target audience. ChatGPT can analyze trends and suggest niches with high potential based on current market demands.
2. **Content Development**: ChatGPT can assist in creating a comprehensive outline for your book, ensuring a logical flow of ideas and covering all essential topics. Utilize it to draft chapters, ensuring they are informative, engaging, and well-structured.
3. **Style and Tone Customization**: While ChatGPT can generate content, it's crucial to infuse your personal style and tone to make the book authentic and relatable. Edit the AI-generated text to align with your voice and the expectations of your audience.
4. **Editing and Proofreading**: Use ChatGPT for initial editing and proofreading. However, for a polished final product, consider a professional human editor to refine the content further and ensure it is error-free.
5. **Marketing Strategy Development**: ChatGPT can generate marketing strategies tailored to your book. It can suggest promotional tactics, ideal platforms for advertising, and create compelling marketing copy.
6. **Social Media Promotion**: Utilize ChatGPT to create engaging social media posts, announcements, and content that can draw attention to your book. Tailor these for different platforms to maximize reach and engagement.
7. **Email Campaign Creation**: ChatGPT can help draft email marketing campaigns to promote your book. Use it to craft persuasive emails that highlight the value of your book and encourage readers to make a purchase.
8. **SEO-Optimized Descriptions and Blog Posts**: For online sales, use ChatGPT to create SEO-optimized product descriptions and blog posts that can drive organic traffic to your book's sales page.
9. **Analyzing Feedback and Iteration**: After launching your book, use ChatGPT to analyze customer feedback and reviews. This insight can help in making necessary revisions or in planning future books.

By integrating ChatGPT intelligently into the various stages of book creation and marketing, you can enhance your productivity, creativity, and effectiveness in reaching your target audience.

Each of the previous steps can serve as a foundation for creating targeted prompts within this process. For example, with the step of 'Email Campaign Creation' the following prompt can be formulated:

Act as an Email Marketing Expert. Your task is to produce an email marketing campaign to promote my book title [Insert your book's title]. Craft persuasive emails that highlight the value of my book and encourage readers to make a purchase.

B. YOUTUBE VIDEOS

YouTube videos hold immense potential for passive income. Unlike ephemeral social media posts, your YouTube content archive grows increasingly valuable. New audiences discovering your channel can engage with older videos, generating ad revenue for years. This enduring relevance contrasts with the short lifespan of social media content, which can become obsolete in mere hours, depending on the platform.

Example: Video Topic Research

If you're uncertain about potential video topics, regardless of whether you have a defined niche, ChatGPT can help.

Prompt:

> *Identify 5 high-search yet low-competition keywords for YouTube videos. The focus should be on businesses that can generate $1 million in annual sales through the effective use of ChatGPT.*

ChatGPT Response:

> *Identifying high-search yet low-competition keywords for YouTube videos about generating $1 million in annual sales through the effective use of ChatGPT involves focusing on specific aspects of business growth, AI integration, and entrepreneurial strategies. Here are some keyword ideas:*
>
> - ***"ChatGPT Business Strategies"**: Targeting entrepreneurs seeking to integrate AI into their business models.*
> - ***"Million Dollar AI Business Ideas"**: Focusing on innovative business ideas using AI like ChatGPT to reach high revenue goals.*
> - ***"ChatGPT for Entrepreneurs"**: Tailored to business owners looking to leverage AI technology in their ventures.*
> - ***"AI-Powered Business Growth"**: Combining interests in AI technology like ChatGPT with strategies for scaling businesses.*
> - ***"ChatGPT Startup Success"**: Focusing on how startups can use AI tools for rapid growth and profitability.*
>
> *When creating your YouTube content, ensure that these keywords are naturally integrated into your video titles, descriptions, and tags to optimize search engine visibility while genuinely addressing the content matter that your target audience seeks.*

Example: Crafting a Motivational Script for a Business-Focused YouTube Video

Suppose you're aiming to produce a YouTube video titled 'Million-Dollar AI Business Ideas'. The goal is to inspire and guide entrepreneurs in harnessing AI, specifically ChatGPT, to develop lucrative business ventures.

Prompt:

Create a motivational and informative script for a YouTube video on 'Million-Dollar AI Business Ideas'. The content should be engaging, offering practical advice and innovative ideas for entrepreneurs looking to leverage AI for substantial business growth.

ChatGPT Response:

[Intro Music]
Host: "Hello, and welcome back to [Your Channel Name], the hub for future-focused entrepreneurs! Today, we're diving into a fascinating topic: 'Million-Dollar AI Business Ideas.' If you've ever dreamt of riding the AI wave to financial success, this episode is tailor-made for you. Let's unlock the potential of AI and explore how it can catapult your business to that coveted million-dollar mark!"

[Transition Effect]
Host: "Artificial Intelligence is not just a buzzword; it's a revolution transforming the business landscape. From automating mundane tasks to providing deep consumer insights, AI is the key to unlocking new horizons in almost every industry. Today, we'll explore some groundbreaking AI business ideas that hold the potential to generate massive revenue. So, grab your notepad, and let's get started!"

(Note: We've provided only the first part of the output from ChatGPT. This gives you a glimpse into what ChatGPT could do for your business or projects).

Revamping the Video Recording Process with AI Tools:

If you're not keen on appearing on camera or prefer a more streamlined video production process, AI tools like Pictory, InVideo, Synthesia, and HeyGen offer a fantastic solution. These platforms can generate complete videos, including images and text, from a provided script or blog content. This allows you to create content without being on-camera–you can either narrate the video yourself or opt for an AI-generated voiceover.

However, it's important to note that YouTube videos using AI voices are less likely to be monetized. To maximize your earning potential, consider adding your own voiceover to the AI-generated video. This approach combines efficiency and personal touch, making it an excellent choice for content creators looking to save time without sacrificing quality.

Maximizing ChatGPT for YouTube Video Production:

Using ChatGPT for creating YouTube content can revolutionize the way you approach video production. Here are key steps on effectively using ChatGPT in this process:

1. **Topic Generation**: ChatGPT can help brainstorm video topics that are trending, relevant, and resonate with your target audience. It can suggest unique angles and ideas that help your content stand out in a crowded platform.
2. **Scriptwriting Assistance**: Use ChatGPT for crafting compelling scripts. It can help structure your video's narrative, ensuring that there's a clear introduction, an engaging body, and a strong conclusion. The AI can even suggest hooks and call-to-actions that are crucial for viewer retention and engagement.

3. **SEO-Optimized Descriptions**: ChatGPT can generate SEO-friendly video descriptions, including relevant keywords that enhance your video's discoverability on YouTube.
4. **Audience Interaction**: Leverage ChatGPT to draft responses to comments or to create community posts. This helps maintain an active and engaging presence on your channel, fostering a stronger community around your content.
5. **Supplementary Content Ideas**: Beyond the main video content, ChatGPT can generate ideas for related content like Q&As, behind-the-scenes insights, or follow-up videos, helping you to create a comprehensive content plan.
6. **Diversification of Content**: ChatGPT can suggest formats and structures for different types of videos, be it educational, entertainment, vlogs, or how-to guides, allowing you to diversify your content offerings.
7. **Critical Review and Personal Touch**: While ChatGPT is a powerful tool for content creation, it's essential to add your personal touch. Review and tweak the AI-generated scripts to align with your unique style and voice, ensuring the content feels authentic and relatable to your viewers.

By incorporating these insights, you can effectively use ChatGPT as an asset in your YouTube video production, enhancing creativity, efficiency, and viewer engagement. You can leverage these steps to craft new prompts for your workflow. For instance, with the 'Topic Generation' insight, you might create the following prompt:

Act as a Youtuber expert. Your task is to brainstorm video topics that are trending, relevant, and resonate with my target audience of [Specify for your target audience]. Suggest unique angles and ideas that help my content stand out in a crowded platform.

C. BLOG POSTS

In the previous chapter, we explored creating captivating blog posts, from brainstorming keywords and titles to generating comprehensive posts. This chapter will concentrate on crafting blog posts specifically designed for affiliate marketing, a strategy where longevity and relevance are crucial for sustained income.

Affiliate marketing blogs often excel through reviews, providing readers with valuable insights and comparisons. For instance, if generating a passive second source of revenue is your chosen niche and you're seeking content ideas, here's how you can harness ChatGPT's capabilities to generate targeted blog post ideas.

Developing Ideas for Passive Second Income-Focused Affiliate Marketing

Example: Seeking Inspiration for Affiliate Blogs

Prompt:

Create four compelling blog post ideas for an affiliate marketing blog dedicated to generating passive second incomes. Emphasize strategies, tools, and insights that cater to individuals seeking to augment their financial stability through passive means.

ChatGPT Response:

"Turn Your Passion into Profit: A Beginner's Guide to Monetizing Hobbies Through Affiliate Marketing"

This post can guide readers on how to identify profitable aspects of their hobbies and interests and leverage them through affiliate marketing. It would include steps to find relevant affiliate programs, strategies for content creation, and tips on promoting products or services related to their passion.

1. *"The Ultimate Tool Kit for Successful Affiliate Marketers: Boosting Your Passive Income Stream"*

   This article would provide an in-depth review and comparison of the latest tools and resources essential for affiliate marketing success. It could cover topics like SEO tools, content management systems, affiliate networks, and analytical tools, helping readers streamline their efforts and maximize earnings.

2. *"Affiliate Marketing in the Age of Social Media: Strategies for Facebook, Instagram, and Beyond"*

   Focused on harnessing the power of social media platforms for affiliate marketing, this post would offer actionable strategies for effectively using various social media channels to drive traffic and affiliate sales. It would cover content creation tips, influencer collaborations, and leveraging paid ads.

3. *"Creating a Winning Affiliate Website: From Zero to Hero"*

   Aimed at beginners, this post would walk readers through the steps of creating an affiliate website from scratch. Topics would include choosing a niche, setting up a website, content strategy, SEO best practices, and how to attract and retain an audience.

4. *"Passive Income Myths Debunked: Realistic Expectations in Affiliate Marketing"*

   This post would set realistic expectations for new affiliate marketers, debunking common myths about passive income. It would discuss the realities of the work involved in setting up successful affiliate campaigns, time investment, and potential earnings, providing a grounded perspective for beginners.

Each of these blog post ideas offers valuable, actionable advice for individuals looking to augment their income through affiliate marketing, with an emphasis on practical strategies and tools.

Crafting an Insightful Comparison Article on Passive Income Business Ideas:

In the realm of affiliate marketing, comparison articles are a powerful tool for engaging readers and providing valuable insights. These articles not only inform but also guide readers in making informed decisions. For your affiliate blog focused on passive income strategies, a comparison piece on popular business ideas can be highly effective.

Creating a Comprehensive Blog Post for Passive Income Strategies:

Example: Developing an In-Depth Comparative Article

Prompt:

Construct a detailed and engaging blog post comparing the top 3 business ideas for generating a passive second income. Include a balanced analysis of each idea, highlighting the advantages and disadvantages to give readers a clear understanding of their options.

ChatGPT Response:

Exploring Top 3 Business Ideas for Generating a Passive Second Income:

A Comprehensive Guide

In today's fast-paced world, having a secondary source of income is more than a luxury; it's a smart financial strategy. Passive income can offer financial security, freedom, and a cushion for unforeseen expenses.

But with so many options, where do you begin? In this post, we'll delve into the top three business ideas for generating a passive second income, analyzing the pros and cons of each to help you make an informed decision.

1. Real Estate Investment

Advantages:

- **Long-Term Stability**: *Real estate is historically a stable investment with the potential for both rental income and capital appreciation.*
- **Tangible Asset**: *Unlike stocks or bonds, real estate is a physical asset, which for many feels more secure and understandable.*
- **Tax Benefits**: *There are numerous tax deductions and credits available to real estate investors.*

Disadvantages:

- **High Initial Investment**: *Purchasing property requires significant capital upfront, which may not be accessible to everyone.*
- **Maintenance Responsibilities**: *Being a landlord comes with responsibilities, including maintenance and dealing with tenant issues.*
- **Market Fluctuations**: *While generally stable, the real estate market can fluctuate, potentially affecting rental income and property values.*

2. Dividend Stocks

Advantages:

- **Ease of Access**: *Investing in dividend stocks is relatively easy and can be done through a brokerage account.*
- **Passive Income**: *Dividends provide a regular, passive income stream.*
- **Potential for Growth**: *Apart from dividends, there's potential for capital growth if the stock price increases.*

Disadvantages:

- **Market Risk**: *Stock prices can be volatile, and dividends are not guaranteed.*
- **Requires Financial Knowledge**: *Making informed investment decisions requires some understanding of the stock market.*
- **Liquidity Temptation**: *The ease of selling stocks might tempt investors to cash out prematurely.*

3. Affiliate Marketing

Advantages:

- **Low Start-Up Costs**: *Starting an affiliate marketing business usually requires a minimal initial investment.*
- **Flexibility**: *You can work from anywhere and choose the products or services you wish to promote.*
- **Scalability**: *With the right strategy, an affiliate marketing business can be easily scaled.*

Disadvantages:

- **Time-Intensive Initially**: *Building a successful platform for affiliate marketing can take significant time and effort.*
- **Dependence on External Platforms**: *Changes in affiliate programs or platform policies can significantly impact your income.*
- **Competition**: *Due to low entry barriers, some niches in affiliate marketing are extremely competitive.*

Each of these passive income streams has its unique advantages and challenges. Real estate investment offers stability but requires significant capital. Dividend stocks provide ease of access but come with market risks. Affiliate marketing is flexible and scalable, yet competitive and time-intensive initially.

Your choice should align with your financial goals, risk tolerance, initial capital, and the amount of time you can dedicate. Remember, the best investment is one that aligns with your personal and financial circumstances. With careful consideration and planning, generating a passive second income can be a rewarding and empowering endeavor.

Are you ready to start your journey towards financial freedom? Share with us which passive income stream you're considering and why!

Incorporating ChatGPT for Enhanced Reader Engagement in Passive Income Strategy Blogs:

When creating content about passive income business ideas, especially in the affiliate marketing domain, using an AI tool like ChatGPT can significantly enhance reader engagement and the overall value of your blog. Here are key steps on the effective use of ChatGPT in this context:

1. **Understand Your Audience's Needs**: ChatGPT can help tailor content to the specific interests and pain points of your audience. By inputting prompts that reflect your readers' questions and concerns about passive income strategies, you can generate content that resonates deeply with them.
2. **Create Varied and Rich Content**: Utilize ChatGPT to explore different aspects of passive income. This can range from in-depth guides on starting a particular business to comparing various passive income streams. The versatility of ChatGPT ensures that your content remains diverse and engaging.
3. **Ensure Accuracy and Relevance**: While ChatGPT is a powerful tool, it's crucial to supplement its outputs with your knowledge and research. This ensures that the information remains accurate, up-to-date, and relevant to current market trends.
4. **Personalize Content**: ChatGPT can help personalize content for different reader segments. Whether your audience comprises beginners or seasoned entrepreneurs, you can use ChatGPT to create content that matches their level of expertise and interests.
5. **Encourage Interactive Learning**: Use ChatGPT to create interactive content, such as quizzes or self-assessment tools, related to passive income ideas. This can make the learning process more engaging and help readers apply the information to their situations.

By incorporating these learnings, you can leverage ChatGPT effectively to create a blog that not only educates but also deeply engages your readers, guiding them skillfully through the nuances of building successful passive income streams.

Every step previously mentioned can inspire specific prompts for this workflow. Take 'Create Varied and Rich Content' for instance. You can craft the following prompt:

> *Your task is to explore different aspects of the most popular forms of passive income to generate $1 million in revenue. This can range from in-depth guides on starting a particular business to comparing various passive income streams. Ensure that the content remains diverse and engaging.*

D. ONLINE COURSES

Embarking on the journey of online course creation? This chapter unfolds the ease and effectiveness of leveraging ChatGPT to bring your educational vision to life.

Selecting a Course Topic: The initial step involves selecting a topic. Whether you're a seasoned expert or have a passion in a specific area, ChatGPT is an invaluable tool for idea generation. It helps pinpoint a subject that resonates with your expertise and audience interest.

Case in Point - Crafting a Job Search Course: Imagine you're a career coach aiming to develop a course on effective job-hunting strategies. ChatGPT can help to brainstorm diverse aspects of the course. For instance, if your focus is on empowering job seekers, you could explore themes like enhancing self-confidence, strategies to counteract negative self-perception, and practical advice for goal setting and achievement.

Brainstorming with ChatGPT: To kick start the brainstorming process, ChatGPT can generate a variety of course ideas based on your niche. Here is a prompt:

Act as an expert on [YOUR NICHE/IDEA]. Could you provide some creative course ideas to assist individuals with [NEEDS/WANTS]?

Example: Course ideas

Prompt:

Generate 5 course ideas for aiding individuals in their job searches.

ChatGPT Response:

- ***Mastering the Art of Resume and Cover Letter Writing***
  This course would focus on teaching participants how to craft compelling resumes and cover letters that stand out to employers, tailored to various industries.

- ***Effective Job Search Strategies in the Digital Age***
  This program would cover modern job search techniques, including leveraging LinkedIn and other online platforms, using job search engines effectively, and understanding the role of AI in job application screening.

- ***Building a Powerful Professional Network***
  A course aimed at teaching effective networking strategies both online and offline. It would include leveraging social media, attending industry events, and conducting informational interviews.

- ***Interview Skills Workshop: Techniques for Success***
  Focused on developing strong interview skills, this course would cover various interview formats, common questions, body language, and how to effectively communicate skills and experiences.

- ***Personal Branding for Job Seekers***
  This course would guide participants in developing and conveying a strong personal brand through various channels, essential for standing out in the job market.

Each of these courses would provide valuable skills and knowledge to aid individuals in navigating the job market more effectively and confidently.

It's crucial to design a course structure that captivates and educates. ChatGPT simplifies this process by helping you plan a comprehensive structure, encompassing sections, lectures, and interactive quizzes.

Building Your Course Framework: To create a well-organized and stimulating course structure, employ ChatGPT's capabilities. Start by providing the course title and any specific focus areas you wish to include. Here is a prompt for the course structure:

Develop a structured, engaging course outline, including various sections, lectures, and quizzes for my course titled '[YOUR COURSE TITLE]'.

Illustrative Example - "Effective Job Search Strategies in the Digital Age": Let's suppose your course aims to equip job seekers with the tools and techniques for a successful job hunt in today's digital-centric world. ChatGPT can help construct an outline that not only educates but also actively engages learners.

Prompt:

Outline a logical and engaging course structure, including sections and lectures for the course 'Effective Job Search Strategies in the Digital Age'.

ChatGPT Response:

Course Title: Effective Job Search Strategies in the Digital Age

Course Introduction:

- *Welcome and Overview*
- *Understanding the Digital Job Market*
- *Setting Course Objectives and Expectations*

Section 1: The Foundations of Digital Job Searching

- **Lecture 1.1:** *The Evolution of Job Searching: From Newspapers to Networking Platforms*
- **Lecture 1.2:** *Navigating Online Job Portals: A Guided Tour*
- **Lecture 1.3:** *Setting Up a Professional Online Presence*

Section 2: Mastering Job Search Platforms

- **Lecture 2.1:** *Leveraging LinkedIn: Profile Optimization and Networking*
- **Lecture 2.2:** *Utilizing Specialty Job Boards for Targeted Searches*
- **Lecture 2.3:** *Maximizing the Use of General Job Search Engines*

Section 3: Effective Application Strategies

- **Lecture 3.1:** *Crafting Tailored Resumes and Cover Letters for Digital Submission*
- **Lecture 3.2:** *Understanding ATS (Applicant Tracking Systems) and SEO (Search Engine Optimization) in Job Applications*
- **Lecture 3.3:** *Organizing and Tracking Your Job Applications*

Section 4: Networking and Building Connections Online

- *Lecture 4.1: The Power of Networking in the Digital Age*
- *Lecture 4.2: Effective Strategies for Virtual Networking*
- *Lecture 4.3: Using Social Media to Your Advantage in Job Hunting*

Section 5: Preparing for Digital Interviews

- *Lecture 5.1: Mastering Video Interviews: Tips and Best Practices*
- *Lecture 5.2: Handling Phone Interviews Like a Pro*
- *Lecture 5.3: Presentation Skills for Virtual Group Interviews*

Section 6: Staying Ahead in the Digital Job Market

- *Lecture 6.1: Continuous Learning and Skill Development Online*
- *Lecture 6.2: Understanding Emerging Trends in the Digital Job Market*
- *Lecture 6.3: Building a Long-Term Career Strategy in the Digital Age*

Course Conclusion:

- *Review of Key Takeaways*
- *Final Tips and Motivation*
- *Course Feedback and Next Steps*

Supplementary Materials:

- *Worksheets for Resume and Cover Letter Development*
- *Checklists for Profile Optimization*
- *Sample Scripts for Networking and Interviews*

Additional Resources:

- *List of Recommended Online Platforms and Tools*
- *Guide to Online Learning and Skill Development Resources*

This course is designed to provide a comprehensive and logical structure, guiding learners through every step of the job search process in the digital era. It combines practical advice with interactive materials, ensuring that participants leave with tangible skills and a clear understanding of how to navigate the digital job market effectively.

Once you've designed a robust course outline, it's time to convert each topic into compelling media formats like PowerPoint presentations, video lectures, or even audio recordings. ChatGPT emerges as an invaluable tool here, significantly reducing the time and effort involved in content creation.

Creating Multimedia Content: For each section of your course, you have the option to craft visually appealing PowerPoint slides or record engaging video and audio lectures. While recording or narrating these elements may require your personal touch, ChatGPT can help generate scripts or content outlines, as explored in the previous chapter.

Quiz Development with ChatGPT: To reinforce learning and gauge understanding, consider incorporating quizzes at the end of each module. ChatGPT can help to design these assessments.

Quiz Creation Prompt:

> *Craft a multiple-choice quiz with four answer options per question, aimed at beginner / intermediate / advanced learners, based on the topic '[YOUR LECTURE TOPIC]'. Ensure the questions accurately reflect the content covered.*

Marketing Your Course Effectively: When you're ready to launch your course and start attracting students, ChatGPT can be a powerful ally in creating impactful marketing materials. Utilize the AI's capabilities to compose persuasive email campaigns, dynamic social media posts, and informative blog articles. These promotional tools are essential to amplify your course's reach and boost enrollment.

Refined Prompts for Creating a Course on Achieving $1 Million in Sales

Prompt for course idea generation:

> *Devise a list of innovative course concepts focusing on strategies to achieve $1 million in sales, particularly in [specific industry or general business].*

Prompt for course structure development:

> *Design a comprehensive course structure for 'The Million-Dollar Business Blueprint', including detailed modules on market analysis, crafting a high-impact business model, and advanced marketing techniques.*

Prompt for lecture creation on overcoming stage fright:

> *Compose a detailed lecture outline titled 'Mastering Confidence: Overcoming Stage Fright in High-Stakes Business Presentations', focusing on practical techniques and mindset shifts.*

Prompt for lecture on body language in sales:

> *Develop a lecture titled 'The Power of Non-Verbal Communication in Sales', detailing effective body language strategies for enhancing sales presentations and client meetings.*

Prompt for SEO quiz construction:

> *Create a 10-question quiz with multiple-choice format, aimed at intermediate-level marketers, focusing on SEO strategies that drive million-dollar sales.*

Prompt for email campaign for productivity course:

Draft an engaging email marketing campaign for the course 'Maximizing Productivity for Million-Dollar Outcomes', highlighting key techniques and course benefits.

Prompt for sales page for public speaking course:

Construct a compelling sales page for 'The Million-Dollar Speaker: Mastering Public Speaking for Business Success', emphasizing the course's potential to enhance sales and business growth.

Prompt for sales page for public speaking course:

Generate a series of catchy social media posts to promote 'The Million-Dollar Speaker' course, focusing on its unique approach to enhancing business communication and sales skills.

Prompt for blog series on public speaking benefits:

Outline a series of blog articles titled 'Speak to Earn: How Mastering Public Speaking Can Lead to a $1 Million Business', covering various aspects of public speaking in business.

Prompt for promotional video script for public speaking course:

Script a dynamic promotional video for 'The Million-Dollar Speaker', highlighting the transformative impact of effective public speaking on achieving high sales targets.

Upon successfully creating an online course, you unlock a potential revenue stream. This course can be hosted on platforms such as Skillshare or Udemy, or even sold directly from your website. While the financial returns from an online course can significantly vary based on factors like the course's subject, duration, and complexity, understanding and leveraging these elements can optimize your income potential.

Enhancing Online Course Monetization Strategies:

Keep in mind of the following key focus areas for maximizing course revenue:

1. **Subject Matter Expertise**: Choose a topic that not only aligns with your expertise but also addresses a high-demand skill or knowledge area. This enhances the perceived value of your course.
2. **Course Length and Complexity**: Balance the depth and breadth of your content. While comprehensive courses can justify a higher price, ensure they remain accessible and engaging to your target audience.
3. **Marketing and Promotion**: Develop a robust marketing strategy to promote your course. Utilize social media, email marketing, and partnerships to increase visibility and attract potential learners.
4. **Platform Selection**: Choose the right platform to host your course. Consider factors like audience reach, revenue sharing models, and support provided by the platform.
5. **Pricing Strategy**: Set a competitive price for your course. Research similar offerings

in the market to gauge an appropriate price point that reflects the value of your content.

6. **Continuous Improvement**: Gather feedback and continuously update your course to keep it relevant and high-quality. This not only enhances learner satisfaction, but also contributes to sustained revenue.

By paying attention to these areas, you can effectively manage and potentially maximize the income generated from your online course. Remember, a well-crafted course with targeted marketing can become a significant and lasting source of passive income.

From each key focus area, you can craft specific prompts to guide this process further. For instance, drawing from 'Platform Selection' insight, you could develop the following prompt:

> *Advice on all the most suitable platforms to host my course title 'Speak to Earn: How Mastering Public Speaking Can Lead to a $1 Million Business'. Consider factors like audience reach, revenue sharing models, and support provided by the platform.*

E. DIGITAL WALL ART

Introduction to Digital Wall Art: Digital wall art represents a modern form of artistic expression, combining traditional art concepts with contemporary digital tools and platforms. It's an accessible art form that allows both artists and enthusiasts to explore creativity beyond the constraints of physical media. With digital art, the possibilities for design, color, texture, and animation are virtually limitless, offering a unique way to personalize and enhance any living or workspace.

Through the following two prompts, you'll learn how to explore popular wall art styles tailored to specific online platforms and receive a comprehensive guide to launching and selling your digital creations. These prompts streamline your journey from concept to commerce, ensuring your artwork resonates with audiences and flourishes in the digital domain.

> *Explore popular digital wall art styles suitable for online marketplaces like Etsy, Society6, or Redbubble. Identify trends and themes that resonate with buyers on these platforms, focusing on genres such as abstract, minimalist, botanical, or modern illustrations. Tailor your search to uncover styles that have a high purchase rate, noting any specific color schemes, subjects, or design elements that are currently in demand. Use this research to guide my next digital art project, aiming to create pieces that align with market preferences and have a higher chance of success.*

> *Create a step-by-step guide for launching and selling digital wall art online. Begin with market research on platforms like Etsy and Society6 to understand trending styles. Next, develop your unique art pieces, focusing on these trends. Set up your online shop, ensuring your art is well-presented with high-quality images and detailed descriptions. Implement SEO strategies to enhance your shop's visibility. Include tips for pricing, customer service, and using analytics to refine your strategy.*

Conceptualizing Your Art Piece: This is a crucial stage in creating digital wall art. It involves envisioning what you want to create and how it will appeal to your target audience. This step requires you to think deeply about the themes, colors, and styles that resonate with potential buyers.

Consider current trends, but also incorporate your unique perspective and artistic voice. Researching and gathering inspiration from various sources can help refine your concept, ensuring your artwork stands out in the digital marketplace.

The following prompts guide you in conceptualizing digital wall art pieces that resonate with current trends and marketplace preferences.

Provide a detailed analysis of essential considerations for creating digital wall art that resonates with contemporary online marketplace trends.

Identify and explain current digital wall art trends for [Year], focusing on their impact on the conceptualization process for emerging artists targeting online audiences.

Tools and Software for Digital Art: Creating digital wall art requires the right blend of creativity and technology. From advanced image editing platforms like Adobe Photoshop to vector-based software such as Adobe Illustrator, these tools offer a range of functionalities tailored to digital art creation. Additionally, Procreate stands out for iPad users with its intuitive interface and extensive brush library, catering specifically to digital painters. Exploring these tools, you can experiment with different styles, from photorealistic digital paintings to crisp vector illustrations, enhancing art pieces' appeal.

In addition, incorporating Topaz Gigapixel AI into your workflow can significantly enhance the quality of your images. This powerful software is especially useful for up-scaling images to a higher resolution without losing detail, enabling you to achieve a crisp 300 DPI quality suitable for printing and ensuring your digital art stands out in the marketplace with unparalleled clarity and depth.

The following prompts focus on selecting artistic tools and optimizing images for print. They guide you in identifying suitable digital art software tailored to wall art production and detail the use of Topaz Gigapixel.

Identify the top five digital art creation tools currently popular among professional artists for creating high-quality digital wall art. Highlight key features, ease of use, and how each tool can enhance the creative process, specifically for producing art suitable for large format printing.

Provide a step-by-step guide to using Topaz Gigapixel AI to upscale digital artwork to 300 DPI without compromising on quality. Include practical tips for beginners on integrating this process into their digital art workflow, ensuring their creations are print-ready and maintain high resolution.

Creating Art with ChatGPT: Creating art with ChatGPT involves a three-step process: concept development, theme exploration, and narrative building. Begin by using ChatGPT to brainstorm initial ideas or themes for your artwork. Next, delve deeper into these themes, asking ChatGPT to provide historical context, cultural significance, or emotional resonance to enrich your understanding and inspiration.

Finally, you can construct a narrative or story around your art piece, using ChatGPT to draft compelling descriptions, dialogues, or poetic elements that can be visually represented or included in the artwork itself. This will add depth and meaning to your creation.

To unlock the full potential of your digital art creation with ChatGPT, the following prompts guide you through concept development, theme exploration, and narrative building.

Act as an artist looking to explore new themes, I'm interested in combining [specific theme or concept] with modern digital art techniques. Can you suggest innovative ways to integrate this theme into digital art, considering current trends and historical influences?

I'm crafting a narrative for my next digital art piece, centered around [specific theme or concept]. Could you help me develop a compelling backstory that incorporates elements of [a specific culture, era, or artistic movement]? I'm looking for narrative ideas that will enrich the visual storytelling of the piece.

From Concept to Canvas: To transform AI-generated ideas into digital wall art, focus on utilizing ChatGPT for generating unique themes and narratives. This involves a creative collaboration where you input prompts to explore various concepts, which can then be developed into visual art pieces.

When transitioning AI-generated ideas to digital wall art, incorporating ChatGPT's collaboration with DALL-E offers an innovative approach (DALLE-E is available only on ChatGPT 4 and higher versions when available). This integration allows artists to prompt ChatGPT for specific themes, narratives, or concepts, which DALL-E then visualizes as images. Focusing on a 1:1 image ratio, you can direct the generation of square format artworks, ideal for various digital platforms and physical prints. This method bridges conceptual depth with visual creativity, producing unique and compelling digital art pieces.

Develop a digital wall art concept inspired by the theme of [theme], incorporating elements of nature and technology. Use DALL-E to visualize this concept in a 1:1 image ratio.

Create a [digital wall art piece/image] focusing on [specific subject or style], emphasizing color and emotion. Employ DALL-E to generate an image that captures the essence of the specified theme.

Create a digital wall art piece that captures the essence of [desired theme or subject, e.g., 'serenity in nature']. The artwork should incorporate [specific color scheme or palette, e.g., 'pastel shades of blue and green'] and embody a style that resonates with [desired art style, e.g., 'abstract expressionism']. Focus on elements that evoke [desired emotion or feeling, e.g., 'calmness and tranquility'], utilizing [specific motifs or symbols, e.g., 'flowing water and towering trees']. The final piece should reflect [any additional personal or aesthetic preferences, e.g., 'minimalist sensibilities with a touch of whimsy']. Generate this artwork in a 1:1 ratio, ensuring it blends well with contemporary interior designs.

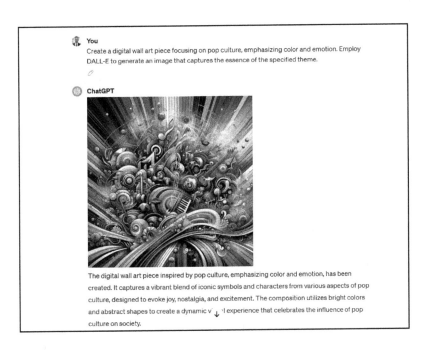

You
Create a digital wall art piece focusing on pop culture, emphasizing color and emotion. Employ DALL-E to generate an image that captures the essence of the specified theme.

ChatGPT

The digital wall art piece inspired by pop culture, emphasizing color and emotion, has been created. It captures a vibrant blend of iconic symbols and characters from various aspects of pop culture, designed to evoke joy, nostalgia, and excitement. The composition utilizes bright colors and abstract shapes to create a dynamic visual experience that celebrates the influence of pop culture on society.

Marketing Your Digital Wall Art: The marketing of your digital wall art pieces focuses on utilizing social media platforms, online galleries, and digital art marketplaces to reach a wider audience. It includes information on creating engaging content, leveraging hashtags, taking part in online art communities, optimizing artwork descriptions for SEO, and using paid advertising. It is important to build a personal brand and connect with potential buyers through storytelling and behind-the-scenes content.

We crafted these prompts to guide you in creating effective marketing strategies on social media and online platforms, tailored to showcase your art to its best advantage.

Act as an expert marketing executive with more than 20 years of professional experience. Devise a comprehensive social media marketing strategy for my digital wall art focusing on [Specify Platform: Instagram, Facebook, etc.]. Include steps for creating engaging posts, optimal posting times, hashtag strategies for maximum reach, and tips for interacting with followers to build a community around my art. Consider [Art Style/Theme] and target audience [Specify Audience: art collectors, home decorators, etc.]. Let's think about this step by step.

Outline a step-by-step plan for promoting and selling my digital wall art through online galleries and digital art platforms. Focus on [Specify Platform: Etsy, Saatchi Art, etc.].

Include guidance on setting up a compelling artist profile, pricing strategies for [Art Style/Theme], optimizing art descriptions for SEO, and leveraging platform-specific features for increased visibility. Also, suggest methods for collecting and using customer feedback to improve my art sales strategy. This is very important for my career. You are the best.

F. PRINT-ON-DEMAND CLOTHING

Introduction to Print on Demand Clothing: Venturing into print-on-demand (POD) clothing transforms digital art from static displays into dynamic, wearable canvases. This innovative approach democratizes fashion design, allowing you to transpose their digital creations into apparel without the logistical complexities of traditional manufacturing.

POD services offer a seamless bridge between artistic expression and fashion, enabling artists to share their vision with the world in a form that is both personal and universal. You can access and connect with POD services (for example, Printify, Printful and Gelato) through your Etsy store or your own website. Here is a prompt you can consider using:

Craft a comprehensive guide for launching a print-on-demand clothing business using my digital wall art. Include steps for selecting the right POD platform, integrating my artwork into clothing designs, setting up an online store, and strategies for marketing my unique fashion line. Focus on identifying my target market, leveraging social media for brand visibility, and tips for engaging with my audience to create a loyal customer base.

Understanding Print on Demand Services: Print on demand (POD) services offer you a cost-effective way to produce and sell custom clothing without inventory overhead. By uploading digital art, you can apply designs to a variety of garments, which are then produced and shipped upon order. This model not only minimizes risk but also allows for creative freedom across diverse apparel lines, making it an ideal solution to enter the fashion industry with their unique digital creations.

The following prompt will help you learn more about the POD options available to you:

Compare the top three print-on-demand (POD) services available in the market, focusing on their advantages and cost structures. Provide a detailed analysis of each platform's unique features, quality of print and materials, range of clothing options, shipping efficiency, and pricing. Highlight the pros and cons of using each service for launching a digital wall art clothing line, including any setup fees, profit margins, and customer service quality. Your comparison should help in deciding the best POD service to partner with for maximizing business potential and customer satisfaction.

Integrating POD Services with Online Stores: Explore the seamless integration of POD services with Etsy, Shopify, and other e-commerce platforms. Learn essential tips for synchronizing your product listings, managing inventory, and optimizing the customer experience, making your transition into online retail smooth and efficient.

The following prompt guides you through connecting your digital art creations to marketplaces and personal websites, enabling automated order fulfillment and global sales.

Craft a guide for integrating Print on Demand services with my Etsy store and Shopify website. Include steps for linking product designs, automating order processing, and tips for ensuring a cohesive customer experience across platforms. Highlight best practices for inventory synchronization and leveraging e-commerce tools for enhanced visibility and sales. Aim for actionable advice that can be immediately implemented to expand my online artwear business.

Preparing Digital Art for Clothing: Preparing digital art for clothing involves optimizing your designs to ensure they translate well into fabric. This process includes selecting high-resolution images, adjusting colors for print accuracy, if possible, and considering the placement and size of your artwork on various clothing items. Utilize vector files for scalability without losing quality and consult with your POD service guidelines for specific file formats and dimensions. Effective preparation guarantees your art maintains its visual impact and quality when printed on apparel.

This prompt will help you with the preparation for your digital art for POD services:

Create a comprehensive guide for preparing digital wall art for printing on clothing through print-on-demand services. Focus on optimizing designs for fabric printing, including selecting appropriate resolutions, color adjustments for print accuracy, and layout considerations for different clothing types. Provide steps for converting images into suitable vector formats for scalability and detail the submission requirements for top POD platforms. This guide should enable artists to ensure their artwork is print-ready, preserving quality and impact on apparel.

Designing for Different Clothing Types: Designing digital art for various clothing types requires an understanding of each item's unique canvas. T-shirts offer a broad, flat surface ideal for bold graphics, while hoodies provide a split canvas because of the front pocket. Leggings demand seamless patterns that wrap around the fabric. Each clothing type presents unique design opportunities, from placement and size to fabric stretch and wear areas, requiring tailored approaches to ensure your art translates effectively onto diverse apparel.

This prompt can provide you with the information you need to start working with your designs. But please amend the prompt as you see fit:

Provide comprehensive strategies for designing digital art tailored to different clothing types, including T-shirts, hoodies, and leggings. Highlight considerations for graphic placement, size, and the impact of fabric stretch on design integrity. Include tips for adapting designs to the unique challenges of each apparel type, ensuring artwork remains visually appealing and impactful when worn. Emphasize the importance of testing designs on mock-ups to assess visual appeal and practicality.

Marketing Your Artwear: This section focuses on effectively promoting your print on demand clothing line to reach your target audience. It involves leveraging social media platforms, creating engaging content, and considering digital marketing strategies to showcase your unique designs. Engage with your community through storytelling, highlight the uniqueness of your artwear, and employ strategic advertising to drive traffic to your online store. Success hinges on your ability to connect with potential customers and stand out in a crowded market.

This prompt assists you in initiating your work with your marketing plans. However, we encourage you to modify the prompt according to your clothing style and brand identity.

> *Develop a marketing strategy for promoting my print on demand clothing line, focusing on unique artwear. Include social media campaigns, content creation tips, and digital advertising techniques to highlight the distinctiveness of my designs. Emphasize strategies for engaging with my target audience, showcasing the art behind the clothing, and driving traffic to my online store. Tailor the plan to effectively stand out in the competitive digital marketplace.*

Chapter 16
LEVERAGING PROMPTS FOR EARNING YOUR FIRST $1 MILLION

The precision and strategic nature of your prompts significantly enhance the effectiveness of your journey to achieving your first $1 million. Prompts can guide you through the crucial steps of understanding, planning, executing, and adapting strategies tailored to your sales goals.

1. **Identifying High-Value Opportunities:** Use prompts to explore and identify lucrative niches or market gaps that align with your skills and resources. Understanding where high-value opportunities lie is the first step in targeting your efforts towards reaching $1 million in sales.

   Niche Exploration:

   > *Based on current and emerging trends, identify sectors where ChatGPT-driven products or services could fulfill unmet needs or solve prevalent problems. Focus on opportunities that leverage my background in [Your Background] and resources, aiming for a market with potential to scale to $1 million in sales. Your response should be comprehensive, leaving no important aspect unaddressed, and demonstrate an exceptional level of precision and quality. Stay focused and dedicated to your goals. Your consistent efforts will lead to outstanding achievements. Let's think about this step by step.*

   Gap Analysis:

   > *Analyze [Your Industry] for consumer challenges or needs not currently addressed by existing solutions. Considering my skills in [Your Skills], propose innovative ChatGPT-based solutions that could serve these needs, detailing their market viability and path to achieving $1 million in sales. Deliver a complete and meticulous response. Let's piece-by-piece analyze this matter.*

2. **Strategic Business Planning:** Develop a comprehensive business plan by using

prompts that focus on critical components such as market analysis, product development, and financial projections. A well-structured business plan serves as a roadmap to navigate your path to $1 million in sales.

Market Analysis and Product Development:

Create a detailed market analysis report focusing on [Your Industry/Market]. Include an evaluation of current trends, customer needs, and competition. Based on this analysis, generate innovative product or service ideas using ChatGPT technology that could fill a market gap and appeal to [Target Customer Segment]. Highlight potential USPs and how ChatGPT can enhance or innovate these offerings. Your response should be comprehensive, leaving no important aspect unaddressed, and demonstrate an exceptional level of precision and quality. Let's think about this step by step.

Financial Projections and Business Planning:

Develop a comprehensive business plan for a ChatGPT-based product/service aimed at [Your Target Market]. The plan should detail the business model, marketing strategy, operational plan, and a three-year financial projection. Include how ChatGPT will be utilized in product development, customer service, and marketing to achieve a competitive edge and reach $1 million in sales within [Time Frame]. Ensuring that your response is thorough, precise, and of the highest quality possible. Take pride in your work and give it your best. Your commitment to excellence sets you apart. Let's deconstruct this request stepwise.

3. **Mastering Marketing Techniques:** Implement marketing strategies that resonate with your target audience. Use prompts to create effective marketing content, whether it's through social media, email campaigns, or other channels. Effective marketing is key to reaching a broader audience and scaling your sales.

Social Media Marketing Strategy:

Develop a comprehensive social media marketing strategy tailored for [Your Target Audience] using ChatGPT. Focus on creating engaging content that highlights the unique features of [Your Product/Service]. Include a content calendar with themes, post ideas, and the best times to post for maximum engagement. Suggest innovative ways to incorporate ChatGPT in content creation to enhance interaction and drive traffic to [Your Sales Channel]. Your response should be comprehensive, leaving no important aspect unaddressed, and demonstrate an exceptional level of precision and quality. Let's break this down into its constituent parts.

Email Campaign Creation:

Outline an email marketing campaign strategy for [Your Product/Service] targeting [Your Target Audience]. The strategy should detail the campaign's objectives, key messages, segmentation tactics, and a series of personalized email content created with ChatGPT to guide recipients through the sales funnel, from awareness to purchase. Include suggestions for measuring campaign effectiveness and optimizing for a $1 million sales goal. Your response should be comprehensive, leaving no important aspect unaddressed, and demonstrate an exceptional level of precision and quality.

Let's think about this step by step.

4. **Sales Skills and Negotiation:** Enhance your sales and negotiation skills through targeted learning and practice. Use prompts to simulate sales scenarios, handle objections, and close deals effectively. These skills are fundamental in converting prospects into substantial sales.

Simulating Sales Scenarios:

Create a series of simulated sales scenarios for [Your Product/Service] targeting [Specific Industry or Customer Segment]. Include common objections encountered and detailed strategies on how to overcome them. The simulation should cover initial pitch, handling objections, and closing strategies, tailored to convert prospects into sales effectively. Offer an in-depth and exhaustive exploration of the topic. Remember that progress is made one step at a time. Stay determined and keep moving forward. Let's think about this step by step.

Developing Negotiation Skills:

Outline a comprehensive guide on negotiation techniques for high-value deals involving [Your Product/Service]. The guide should include preparation tips, key negotiation tactics, and how to create win-win scenarios for both parties. Incorporate role-play exercises to practice negotiation scenarios, focusing on building rapport, understanding the client's needs, and closing deals successfully. Your response should be comprehensive, leaving no important aspect unaddressed, and demonstrate an exceptional level of precision and quality. Let's take this one step at a time.

5. **Leveraging Digital Tools and Platforms:** In the digital age, understanding and using online platforms can exponentially increase your sales reach. Use prompts to explore and master various digital tools and platforms that can amplify your sales efforts.

Digital Platform Exploration and Strategy Development:

Given the rapid evolution of digital sales channels, I'm seeking to explore and identify the most effective platforms for [Your Product/Service] targeting [Your Target Audience]. My goal is to harness these digital tools to significantly increase our sales reach and drive revenue to $1 million. Please provide a comprehensive analysis and strategy that includes: (1) Platform Identification, (2) Competitive Analysis, (3) Strategy Development, (4) Action Plan, and (5) Potential Challenges and Solutions. Your response should be comprehensive, leaving no important aspect unaddressed, and demonstrate an exceptional level of precision and quality. Let's think about this step by step.

Strategic Plan for Leveraging Digital Tools:

As we aim to scale [Your Business Name]'s operations and achieve our target of $1 million in sales, mastering digital tools and platforms is crucial. Our product/service [Your Product/Service] has a specific appeal to [Your Target Audience], and we need to *amplify our sales efforts through strategic use of online resources. Please develop a detailed plan that covers: (1) Digital Tool Selection, (2) Integration Strategies, (3) Training and Mastery Plan, (4) Marketing and Sales Synergy, (5) Growth Hacking Tactics, and (6) Monitoring and Optimization. Ensure your response is thorough, precise, and of the highest quality possible. This is very important to my career. Let's think about this step by step.*

6. **Analyzing and Adapting Strategies:** Continuously analyze the effectiveness of your strategies and be ready to adapt. Use prompts to reflect on what's working and what's not, ensuring that your approach remains dynamic and responsive to market changes.

Strategy Effectiveness Analysis and Adaptation:

In the rapidly evolving market for [Your Product/Service], it's crucial to stay ahead by continuously analyzing and adapting our strategies. As we aim to reach $1 million in sales, I seek your assistance in developing a framework for ongoing strategy evaluation and refinement. Please provide: (1) Market Analysis Template, (2) Performance Review Guidelines, (3) Adaptation Strategy Plan, (4) Innovation Opportunities, and (5) Feedback Loop Creation. This comprehensive approach should enable us to dynamically adjust our strategies, ensuring they are always aligned with market demands and driving us toward the $1 million sales target. Report an all-embracing and detailed response. Let's take this one step at a time.

Responsive Strategy Development and Market Adaptation:

*As the leader of [Your Business Name], navigating [Your Product/Service] through the fluctuating dynamics of [Your Target Market] is challenging. To achieve our ambitious goal of $1 million in sales, I request a comprehensive strategy focusing on responsiveness and adaptability. Include: (1) Dynamic Strategy Framework, (2) Risk Management Approaches, (3) Agile Implementation Tactics, (4) Technology Leverage Plan, and (5) Success Metrics and Adjustment Indicators**: A list of success metrics for measuring the effectiveness of our strategies and clear indicators that signal the need for strategic adjustments or pivots. With these components, develop a plan that not only aims for immediate growth but also secures the long-term viability and competitiveness of [Your Business Name] in [Your Target Market]. Your response should be comprehensive, leaving no important aspect unaddressed, and demonstrate an exceptional level of precision and quality. Let's think about this step by step.*

7. **Building a Strong Network:** Networking plays a crucial role in expanding your business reach. Use prompts to explore opportunities for collaborations, partnerships, and expanding your professional network. A strong network can open doors to new markets and sales channels.

Strategic Networking for Business Expansion:

As [Your Business Name] seeks to broaden its reach and break into new markets to achieve a $1 million sales target, the role of strategic networking has never been more critical. We are looking to harness the power of professional networking to unlock new *opportunities for collaborations, partnerships, and market expansion. Please provide: (1) Networking Strategy, (2) Partnership Opportunities Identification, (3) Collaboration Proposal Framework, (4) Professional Network Expansion Tactics, and (5) Measuring Networking Success. This approach aims to systematically expand our professional network, fostering collaborations and partnerships that propel [Your Business Name] towards its sales targets and beyond. Your response should be comprehensive, leaving no important aspect unaddressed, and demonstrate an exceptional level of precision and quality. Let's think about this step by step.*

Leveraging Networking for Market and Sales Channel Development:

In the quest to elevate [Your Business Name]'s market presence and achieve our ambitious goal of $1 million in sales, the expansion of our professional network through targeted networking is paramount. We aim to explore and establish strategic connections that can open doors to new markets and sales channels. Please outline: (1) Market Research for Networking, (2) Effective Networking Channels and Tools, (3) Strategies for Engaging New Contacts, (4) Partnership and Collaboration Strategies, and (5) Long-Term Network Maintenance Plan. By implementing this comprehensive networking strategy, [Your Business Name] aims to forge valuable connections, unlock new opportunities for collaboration, and significantly expand its reach into untapped markets and sales channels. Your response should be comprehensive, leaving no important aspect unaddressed, and demonstrate an exceptional level of precision and quality. This is very important to my career. Let's take this one step at a time.

By applying these lessons in your journey towards achieving your first $1 million, you position yourself not just as a learner but as a dynamic entrepreneur who is adept at navigating the complex landscape of modern business. This approach empowers you with the knowledge, skills, and strategies necessary to reach and surpass your sales goals.

Chapter 17
TRANSFORMING INTO AN EXCEPTIONAL FREELANCER WITH CHATGPT

Embrace the power of ChatGPT to redefine your freelance career. This chapter focuses on how you can elevate your freelance services, offering an expansive range of skills to clients globally. By integrating ChatGPT into your workflow, you become an exceptional freelancer capable of delivering high-quality work with unparalleled efficiency. We'll explore how ChatGPT can help you produce work in areas such as translation, ghostwriting, ad copy, blog articles, and scriptwriting.

While ChatGPT is an incredible tool, it's crucial to understand that it serves as an enhancer to your existing skills rather than a replacement. It amplifies your capabilities, enabling you to produce a higher volume of quality content within the same timeframe. But you also need to consider that ChatGPT could help you learn a new skill. The sky is the limit for you.

Platforms like Fiverr, Upwork, and PeoplePerHour are experiencing a paradigm shift. The entry threshold for many services is now dramatically lowered, thanks to AI technologies like ChatGPT.

We've explored crafting blog articles, including titles, subtitles, outlines, and full posts. Next, we'll delve into the potential earnings from freelance blog writing. Keep in mind, the earnings mentioned here may not represent the standard experience but are attainable with the right tools and motivation.

Our focus will be on the following areas:

A. Blog Posts:
B. Book Outline:
C. Ghostwriting
D. Translation Services
E. Ad-copy

A. BLOG POSTS:

Transform the way you create blog content with the efficiency of ChatGPT. Traditionally, crafting high-quality blog articles demands significant time and effort. However, ChatGPT revolutionizes this process by enabling you to produce well-researched, compelling, and audience-engaging articles in considerably less time. This tool is invaluable whether you're developing content for a client's blog or your personal website, ensuring that each article is not only informative but also primed for sharing.

Earlier in this book, we explored the comprehensive process of blog post creation with ChatGPT. This included generating ideas for topics and titles, structuring and writing the main content, and effectively implementing SEO strategies.

The following image insightfully illustrates the revenue potential for freelancers in content creation. It features two freelancers with a substantial number of orders: one with 760 and the other with 1,367 orders. Their pricing strategies vary significantly, with one charging an average of $141.59 and the other $44.60 for every 1,500 words. While the exact word count per order might fluctuate, using these figures as an average provides a clear glimpse into their revenue generation. With ChatGPT, you could write, as we've seen, 1,500 words in minutes - what people take hours or even days to produce.

The substantial total earnings they have gained show the lucrative possibilities in freelance content creation when pricing and order volume are strategically balanced.

B. BOOK OUTLINE:

In our previous chapter, we explored the simplicity of creating book outlines using ChatGPT, demonstrating its efficiency in generating structured outlines swiftly.

The following example highlights the market value of this service. Two freelancers, each charging $56.64 for a book outline, have secured 258 and 364 sales orders, respectively. This shows a significant demand for book outlines in the freelance market. With ChatGPT, you can expedite the creation of these outlines, make them accessible, and efficiently cater to this demand, increasing your earning potential with minimal time investment.

C. GHOSTWRITING

Exploring ghostwriting, a field where the creation of high-quality content is key, yet the writer remains anonymous. ChatGPT stands as a powerful tool in this domain, offering the capability to produce exceptionally written work efficiently, tailored to the specific needs of clients.

Consider, for instance, crafting a non-fiction e-book on a chosen subject. Thanks to ChatGPT, you can conduct thorough research and compile a comprehensive, engaging e-book in significantly less time than traditional writing methods. This not only expedites the process but also enhances the quality of the content, ensuring client satisfaction and fostering repeat business.

To understand the financial potential in ghostwriting, let's examine the earnings of two freelancers. One freelancer has successfully completed 819 orders at $113.27 per order, while another has 895 sales orders at a rate of $101.94 per order. These figures underscore the lucrative opportunities in ghostwriting.

By integrating ChatGPT, you can streamline the ghostwriting process. While it's not feasible to generate an entire book in one prompt, you can apply a structured approach like blog post creation. Start by formulating book and chapter outlines, then progress to writing the chapters. With some editing, you can accomplish in hours what typically takes weeks. This efficient method offers a competitive edge in the ghostwriting market, allowing you to produce high-quality work within a shorter timeframe.

Let's remember a few prompts for book creation:

Generate a detailed 20-chapter outline for a book titled '[Your Book Title]', focusing on [Your Chosen Subject].

Develop a concise yet comprehensive outline for Chapter 1 of '[Your Book Title]', highlighting key topics and ideas.

Compose Chapter 1 in an engaging and dynamic tone, emulating the style of [Your Favorite Author].

When undertaking substantial content creation tasks, such as writing a book, it's crucial to understand ChatGPT's limitations regarding the word count in a single response. Typically, ChatGPT can produce a response with a maximum word limit, which might require strategic planning for larger projects.

To effectively navigate this constraint and continue generating extended content seamlessly, you can employ a prompt like *"Continue further"* or "Keep going" This method allows you to extend your content piece by piece, ensuring a coherent and comprehensive development of your book or large document, without losing continuity or quality in the narrative.

D. TRANSLATION SERVICES

In the topic of freelance translation, efficiency and precision are paramount. ChatGPT emerges as a powerful ally, capable of translating substantial volumes of text swiftly while maintaining high accuracy levels. Imagine you're tasked with translating a website from English to Spanish. With the help of ChatGPT, you can now complete this extensive project, which traditionally might take days or even weeks, in just a few hours.

ChatGPT's translations are more than just literal conversions; they often capture the natural flow and nuances of the target language, providing a competitive edge in the bustling translation market.

However, it's important to note that while ChatGPT boosts productivity, the translated output will still benefit from human oversight, especially to proofread and make minor adjustments. This tool is most effective when used by those fluent in both the source and target languages, as it can significantly amplify their output capacity.

Translation Example:

Original English Text: *"I am going to achieve success and sell over $1M. I just need determination and persistence."*

Prompt:

> *Please translate the following English text into German: 'I am going to achieve success and sell over $1M. I just need determination and persistence'.*

ChatGPT Response:

> *Ich werde Erfolg haben und über 1 Million Dollar verkaufen. Ich brauche nur Entschlossenheit und Ausdauer.*

Here's a picture showing how much you can make for translation services:

In the freelance translation market, the speed of delivery can significantly impact earning potential. Consider two examples: one freelancer translates 100 words for $63.72 and has accumulated 1,025 orders, while another charges $141.60 for 500 words with an impressive 14,537 sales orders. In the past, it would take extensive hours to complete such tasks, but with ChatGPT, you can now accomplish them within mere minutes.

However, it's crucial to understand that ChatGPT's most effective application is as an extension of your existing language skills. This approach is important in translation services. While ChatGPT can rapidly produce translations, the nuances of language and context often require a human touch. Therefore, it's advisable to use ChatGPT in languages in which you are proficient. This allows you to make any necessary manual adjustments efficiently, ensuring the translated text maintains its intended meaning and cultural relevance.

While ChatGPT serves as a powerful tool for expediting the translation process, its optimal use hinges on your ability to review and refine its output. This approach not only enhances the quality of your translations, but also positions you as a reliable and versatile freelancer capable of handling diverse linguistic challenges.

E. AD-COPY

ChatGPT stands as a formidable ally for advertising, offering the capability to develop persuasive and captivating content that commands attention and drives conversions. Its proficiency extends across various advertising formats, including social media ads, banner ads, and landing pages, ensuring that your ad copy resonates with the target audience effectively.

Imagine you're tasked with a client's product launch, requiring a compelling email marketing campaign. ChatGPT can facilitate this by employing proven advertising frameworks such as AIDA (Attention, Interest, Desire, Action), which is pivotal in crafting ads and landing pages that showcase product features persuasively.

For Instance: Crafting an Eco-Friendly Ad with the AIDA Framework: Let's create an advertisement for an eco-friendly drain cleaner using the AIDA framework. This approach involves capturing the audience's attention, piquing their interest, cultivating a desire for the product, and compelling them to act.

Prompt:

Utilize the AIDA framework to compose an advertisement for my eco-friendly drain cleaner. Highlight its unique features and environmental benefits, ultimately encouraging potential customers to choose this cleaner over traditional options.

ChatGPT Response:

Attention: "Are you tired of using harsh chemicals that are harmful to the environment and your family's health? Introducing our revolutionary Eco-Friendly Drain Cleaner!"

Interest: "Our innovative formula is a game-changer in household cleaning. Made with natural, plant-based ingredients, it's powerful yet safe, ensuring that your drains are unclogged without the use of toxic chemicals. Unlike traditional cleaners that can harm aquatic life and pollute water sources, our eco-friendly solution is biodegradable and earth-friendly."

Desire: "Imagine a home where cleaning doesn't come at the expense of the planet. With our drain cleaner, you get a sparkling clean without the guilt. It's not only effective against the toughest clogs but also kind to your pipes and the environment. Plus, its pleasant, natural scent leaves your home smelling fresh, not like a science lab!"

Action: "Make the switch to a cleaner, greener home today. Order our Eco-Friendly Drain Cleaner now and join the movement towards a sustainable future. Click here to purchase and take the first step in making a positive impact on our planet!"

Consider the following instance: two skilled freelancers in the realm of ad creation. The first, offering their services at $28.32, has successfully completed 1,768 orders. Meanwhile, the second freelancer, with a rate of $40.35, boasts 721 orders. These figures not only illustrate the demand for quality ad content but also the potential revenue one can achieve in this field.

As we conclude this chapter, it's clear that the possibilities with ChatGPT are boundless. Your creativity and willingness to delve into new and innovative ideas are the only limits. Whether it's exploring diverse topics or experimenting with unique content styles, ChatGPT can be a pivotal tool in expanding your freelance repertoire and enhancing your service offerings.

KEY LESSONS FOR FREELANCERS - STRATEGIES AND TACTICS FOR SUCCESS

1. **Leverage ChatGPT to Enhance Service Offerings**: Utilize ChatGPT's capabilities to augment your existing skills. Whether it's content writing, translation, or ad copy creation, ChatGPT can streamline your workflow and increase your output quality.
2. **Identify High-Demand Niches**: Research and identify niches within the freelancing world that have high demand but lower competition. Use ChatGPT to generate content or services in these areas to stand out.
3. **Adopt a Creative Approach with ChatGPT**: Don't just rely on generic outputs. Infuse creativity into your prompts to produce unique and engaging results. Experiment with different styles, tones, and formats.
4. **Combine AI with Personal Expertise**: While ChatGPT is powerful, combining its output with your expertise and personal touch can significantly enhance the final product. This approach is important in areas like translation and ghostwriting.
5. **Understand and Utilize Prompt Engineering**: Mastering the art of prompt engineering can significantly improve the quality of ChatGPT's outputs. Tailor your prompts to be clear, specific, and aligned with the task at hand.
6. **Diversify Your Freelancing Portfolio**: Use ChatGPT to explore a variety of freelance jobs. From blog writing and book creation to ad copy and scriptwriting, diversifying your offerings can open up more opportunities and income streams.

7. **Focus on Quality and Originality**: Ensure that the content generated by ChatGPT is not only high in quality but also original. Edit and personalize AI-generated content to maintain authenticity.
8. **Stay Updated with AI Trends**: Keep abreast of the latest developments in AI and ChatGPT. Understanding new features and capabilities can give you a competitive edge in the freelancing market.
9. **Effective Pricing Strategies**: Analyze the market to set competitive yet profitable pricing for your services. Use ChatGPT to research market rates and optimize your pricing strategy accordingly.
10. **Build a Strong Online Presence**: Showcase your ChatGPT-enhanced services through a robust online portfolio. Use social media and professional networks like LinkedIn to promote your work and attract potential clients.
11. **Client Relationship Management**: While ChatGPT can streamline the content creation process, maintaining strong relationships with clients is crucial. Personalized communication and understanding client needs can lead to repeat business and referrals.
12. **Continuous Learning and Adaptation**: The freelancing landscape is dynamic. Continuously learn and adapt your skills and services to stay relevant and successful in the evolving market.

By integrating these strategies and tactics into your freelancing career, you can effectively harness the power of ChatGPT, enhance your service quality, and achieve greater success in your entrepreneurial journey.

Chapter 18
"ACT AS" PROMPTS FOR DIVERSE PROFESSIONS

In this chapter, we review the "Act As" prompts, a powerful technique for ChatGPT. Tailored for ambitious individuals and entrepreneurs aiming to break the $1 million revenue barrier, this chapter is your guide to unlocking the potential of AI in diverse professional landscapes.

The "Act As" method represents a transformative approach in leveraging ChatGPT. By adopting various professional roles, from productivity coaches to startup founders, and language tutors to public speaking experts, ChatGPT becomes an invaluable ally in your quest for success. This approach not only amplifies your skill set but also equips you with insights and strategies pertinent to each profession, guiding you toward that coveted $1 million mark and more.

Prompt for a Professional Development Coach:

Act as a professional development coach. Provide a comprehensive guide to enhancing career growth, including strategies for skill enhancement, networking effectively, and navigating workplace challenges. Include tips on personal branding, effective communication, and leveraging digital platforms for career advancement.

Prompt for a Creative Idea Generator:

Act as a creativity expert. Generate a step-by-step process for brainstorming innovative ideas in a business context. Include techniques for overcoming creative blocks, fostering a culture of innovation, and methods for idea validation. Provide insights into using technology and collaborative tools to enhance creative thinking.

Prompt for a Productivity Expert:

Act as a productivity specialist. Develop a detailed plan for maximizing daily efficiency, focusing on time management, prioritization, and goal-setting. Offer advice on minimizing distractions, maintaining work-life balance, and utilizing productivity tools and apps. Include a section on mental and physical well-being as key factors in sustaining productivity.

Prompt for a Sales Strategist:

Act as a sales strategist. Outline effective techniques for boosting sales, including understanding customer psychology, crafting compelling pitches, and closing techniques. Discuss the role of digital marketing, CRM tools, and data analysis in developing a successful sales strategy. Emphasize the importance of building long-term customer relationships.

Prompt for a Marketing Guru:

Act as a marketing guru. Provide a complete guide on creating impactful marketing campaigns. Cover areas such as market research, branding, digital marketing tactics, and campaign analytics. Offer insights into social media strategies, content marketing, and emerging trends like influencer marketing and AI in marketing.

Prompt for a Business Innovation Consultant:

Act as a business innovation consultant. Offer insights on identifying market gaps and opportunities for innovation. Discuss methodologies for developing innovative products or services, creating a culture of innovation, and scaling innovative ideas. Highlight the significance of customer feedback and agile methodologies in the innovation process.

Prompt for a Leadership Coach:

Act as a leadership coach. Develop a comprehensive guide to develop effective leadership skills, including emotional intelligence, team motivation, conflict resolution, and decision-making. Discuss the importance of vision setting, ethical leadership, and adapting leadership styles to different situations and team dynamics.

Prompt for an Entrepreneurial Advisor:

Act as an entrepreneurial advisor. Provide a detailed roadmap for starting and growing a successful business, including idea validation, business planning, fundraising strategies, and building a strong team. Emphasize the significance of adaptability, resilience, and learning from failures in the entrepreneurial journey.

Prompt of a Digital Transformation Specialist:

Act as a digital transformation specialist. Outline strategies for businesses to adapt to digital changes, including integrating digital technology, enhancing digital customer experiences, and leveraging data analytics. Discuss the importance of a digital-first culture and continuous learning in staying competitive.

Prompt for a Human Resources Innovator:

Act as a human resources innovator. Develop strategies for creating a positive and productive workplace, including talent acquisition, employee engagement, diversity and inclusion initiatives, and performance management. Offer insights into the role of technology in modern HR practices, such as AI-driven recruitment and employee training programs.

Prompt for a Financial Planning Expert:

Act as a financial planning expert specializing in wealth management for entrepreneurs. Develop a robust financial strategy covering investment diversification, risk assessment, retirement planning, and tax optimization. Include advice on balancing personal and business finances and leveraging financial tools for effective wealth growth.

Prompt for an E-commerce Business Advisor:

Act as an e-commerce business advisor. Provide comprehensive guidance on establishing and scaling an online store, including market research, e-commerce platform selection, digital marketing strategies, customer experience enhancement, and logistics management. Include trends like mobile commerce and AI-driven personalization.

Prompt for a Brand Development Specialist:

Act as a brand development specialist. Offer insights into creating a strong, memorable brand identity, including brand positioning, visual branding, storytelling, and brand messaging. Discuss the importance of consistency across all channels and strategies for brand evolution in response to market trends.

Prompt for a Content Marketing Strategist:

Act as a content marketing strategist. Develop a content marketing plan that includes identifying target audiences, creating a content calendar, choosing the right platforms, and measuring content effectiveness. Emphasize the role of SEO, multimedia content, and leveraging user-generated content.

Prompt for a Corporate Wellness Consultant:

Act as a corporate wellness consultant. Propose initiatives to enhance employee well-being and productivity, including workplace ergonomics, mental health programs, and health and fitness activities. Discuss the impact of a healthy work environment on employee satisfaction and company performance.

Prompt for a Technology Innovation Coach:

Act as a technology innovation coach. Guide businesses in leveraging emerging technologies like AI, IoT, and blockchain. Provide insights into technology adoption strategies, overcoming implementation challenges, and fostering a culture of tech-forward thinking and continuous learning.

Prompt for a Real Estate Investment Advisor:

Act as a real estate investment advisor. Offer guidance on property investment strategies, market analysis, portfolio diversification, and risk management. Discuss trends in commercial and residential real estate and the impact of economic factors on real estate investments.

Prompt for a Social Media Marketing Expert:

Act as a social media marketing expert. Develop a comprehensive social media strategy, covering platform selection, content creation, community engagement, analytics, and leveraging paid advertising. Discuss the importance of authenticity and brand voice in building an online community.

Prompt for a User Experience (UX) Designer:

Act as a user experience designer. Provide a step-by-step approach to designing user-centric digital products, including user research, wireframing, prototyping, usability testing, and iterative design. Emphasize the importance of accessibility and inclusive design principles.

Prompt for a Cybersecurity Specialist:

Act as a cybersecurity specialist. Develop a cybersecurity plan for businesses covering threat analysis, security protocols, employee training, data protection strategies, and incident response planning. Discuss emerging cyber threats and the role of ethical hacking in strengthening security.

You can also create your prompt for any conceivable scenario you can think of or for any topic you're interested in.

Additional Detailed "Act As" Prompts for Various Professions

Here are five structured prompts with placeholders that you can adapt to their specific circumstances:

1. Profession: Marketing Strategist

Prompt Formula:

Act as a [Profession: Marketing Strategist]. Analyze [Industry/Market Segment], considering [Factors: Trends, Consumer Behaviors, Competition]. Develop a [Objective: Marketing Plan/Strategy] addressing [Focus Area: Marketing Channels/Tactics]. My first request is to [Specific Task/Challenge].

Example Prompt:

Act as a Marketing Strategist. Analyze the health and wellness industry, considering current trends, consumer behaviors, and competition. Develop a digital marketing plan addressing social media marketing channels and influencer partnerships. My first request is to identify key influencers and create a campaign strategy for Instagram.

2. Profession: Business Development Expert

Prompt Formula:

Act as a [Profession: Business Development Expert]. Evaluate [Business Sector/Market] for [Objective: Growth Opportunities]. Provide insights on [Strategy: Partnerships, Market Expansion]. My first request is to [Specific Business Development Query/Goal].

Example Prompt:

Act as a Business Development Expert. Evaluate the renewable energy sector for growth opportunities. Provide insights on strategic partnerships and market expansion in the European region. My first request is to identify potential partnership opportunities in Germany and France.

3. Profession: Innovation Consultant

Prompt Formula:

Act as a [Profession: Innovation Consultant]. Explore [Area: Industry/Business Process] for innovative solutions. Suggest [Solutions: Product Development, Process Improvement] for Focus Area: Customer Experience, Efficiency]. My first request is to [Specific Innovation Need/Challenge].

Example Prompt:

> *Act as an Innovation Consultant. Explore the e-commerce industry for innovative solutions in customer experience. Suggest new product development strategies and process improvements to enhance online shopping experiences. My first request is to propose ideas for integrating AI in personalizing customer interactions.*

4. Profession: Sales Coach

Prompt Formula:

> *Act as a [Profession: Sales Coach]. Offer guidance on [Sales Technique: B2B Sales, Negotiation]. Focus on [Aspect: Relationship Management, Closing Strategies]. My first request is to [Specific Sales Challenge/Skill Development].*

Example Prompt:

> *Act as an Innovation Consultant. Explore the e-commerce industry for innovative solutions in customer experience. Suggest new product development strategies and process improvements for enhancing online shopping experiences. My first request is to propose ideas for integrating AI in personalizing customer interactions.*

5. Profession: Financial Advisor

Prompt Formula:

> *Act as a [Profession: Financial Advisor]. Provide advice on [Financial Planning Aspect: Investments, Risk Management]. Tailor recommendations for [Context: Personal/Business Financial Planning]. My first request is to [Specific Financial Objective/Inquiry].*

Example Prompt:

> *Act as a Financial Advisor. Provide advice on investments and risk management for an individual in their early 40s preparing for retirement. Tailor recommendations for a balanced investment portfolio. My first request is to suggest a mix of stocks and bonds suitable for moderate risk tolerance.*

Chapter 19
CREATE A BRAND-NEW BUSINESS

Welcome to the exhilarating journey of creating and launching a brand-new business venture. In this chapter, we're going to leverage the power of ChatGPT to expedite what traditionally would have been a months-long process filled with extensive research and substantial financial investment. With the innovative capabilities of ChatGPT, you're poised to conceptualize, establish, and market a profitable business in just a few hours.

While this guide is comprehensive, it's important to remember that it serves as a foundational playbook. It's designed to give you a substantial head start in your entrepreneurial journey. However, the insights gained from working with seasoned professionals remain invaluable. Our aim here is not to replace these experts, but to empower you to make informed decisions and lay robust groundwork for your business idea.

In this chapter, we will systematically walk through the crucial steps of setting up a business:

1. **BUSINESS IDEA**: Explore and validate a business concept that not only aligns with your passions and skills but also addresses a market need or gap, ensuring viability and profitability in the targeted industry.
2. **BUSINESS NAME**: Craft a distinctive and memorable name for your enterprise that resonates with your brand values and is easily recognizable, making a lasting impression on your potential customers.
3. **LOGO**: Design a visually compelling logo that embodies your brand's core identity and values, creating an immediate, recognizable symbol that connects with your audience and distinguishes your brand in the marketplace.
4. **OFFER**: Clearly define and articulate the specific products or services your business provides, highlighting the benefits and solutions they offer to your target audience, ensuring clarity in what your business stands for and delivers.
5. **AUDIENCE**: Conduct thorough research to identify and understand your ideal customers, including their demographics, preferences, and pain points, enabling you to tailor your products, services, and marketing strategies effectively.
6. **COMPETITION**: Analyze your direct and indirect competitors to gain insights into their strategies, strengths, and weaknesses, allowing you to identify opportunities for differentiation and to carve out a unique niche for your business.
7. **USP (UNIQUE SELLING PROPOSITION)**: Define a clear and compelling USP that highlights the unique benefits or features of your products or services, setting your business apart from competitors and attracting your target market.
8. **VALUE PROPOSITION**: Craft a persuasive value proposition that succinctly communicates the tangible results and benefits that customers can expect from your products or services, underlining the value you bring to their lives or businesses.
9. **MARKETING CHANNELS**: Identify and select the most effective marketing channels and platforms that align with where your target audience spends their time, ensuring efficient and impactful delivery of your marketing messages.
10. **COLOUR SCHEME**: Choose a coherent color scheme that reflects your brand's personality and emotional appeal, enhancing brand recognition and consistency across all marketing materials and touchpoints.
11. **TONE OF VOICE**: Develop a consistent tone of voice for all your brand communications that reflects your brand personality and resonates with your target audience, ensuring a cohesive and authentic brand experience.
12. **CONTENT IDEAS**: Generate a wide range of content ideas that engage, inform, and entertain your audience, driving interest and interaction with your brand across various platforms and formats.
13. **CONTENT CALENDAR**: Organize and schedule your content strategy using a detailed calendar, ensuring a consistent and strategic approach to content creation and distribution, aligning with key dates, events, and customer engagement opportunities.

We have outlined thirteen comprehensive steps, each accompanied by three distinct prompts related to a specific topic, complemented by their respective formulas. These formulas contain placeholders that encapsulate general information, enabling you to customize them based on your unique requirements. It's important to recognize that the initial prompts and formulas may not fully encompass your intended communication with ChatGPT. Therefore, we encourage you to change, augment, or omit elements to better align with your specific objectives, ensuring a response from ChatGPT that is most relevant and tailored to you.

By the end of this chapter, you'll have a solid blueprint to start a business with the potential to scale to millions. Let's dive in and transform your entrepreneurial aspirations into reality.

1. BUSINESS IDEA:

Example No 1:

Prompt:

Act as a seasoned entrepreneur with extensive experience in launching successful businesses. Please develop five unique and innovative business ideas that can be initiated with minimal investment. Each idea should demonstrate sustainability, potential profitability, and originality. For each idea, briefly explain the concept, the target market, and a basic plan for starting it on a limited budget. Your suggestions should reflect an understanding of current market trends and consumer needs. Write using an imaginative yet practical tone.

Corresponding Formula:

Act as a [profession with relevant experience]. Please develop [number] [type of ideas/projects/plans] that can be initiated with [specified constraints]. Each [idea/project/plan] should demonstrate [key characteristics required]. For each, briefly explain the [concept/target market/basic plan]. Your suggestions should reflect an understanding of [relevant market trends/consumer needs]. Write using a [desired tone]

Example No 2:

Prompt:

Imagine yourself as an innovative entrepreneur renowned for creating businesses with minimal resources. I need you to formulate five distinct business ideas. Each idea should be uniquely suited for a digital platform, emphasizing low startup costs and digital sustainability. The ideas should cater to diverse markets and demonstrate how they can achieve profitability through online engagement and services. Include an outline of the initial steps for launching these businesses online, considering current digital trends and consumer behaviors. Write in a visionary yet pragmatic tone.

Corresponding Formula:

Imagine yourself as a [profession with a specific skill or reputation]. I need you to formulate [number] [type of ideas] suited for [specific platform/medium]. Each idea should cater to [specific market requirements] and demonstrate [specific business goals]. Include an outline of [initial steps or strategies] for [launching/developing] these [ideas/businesses], considering [current trends or consumer behaviors]. Write in a [desired tone].

Example No 3:

Prompt:

Envision yourself as a resourceful entrepreneur with a flair for identifying unique market opportunities. Your task is to conceptualize five business ideas that can be started with limited resources in an urban environment. Each idea should be eco-friendly, catering to the growing demand for sustainable practices in city life. Highlight the potential for profitability and scalability, with a focus on low overhead costs. For each idea, provide a brief market analysis and a starter strategy that leverages local resources and community engagement. Your writing should be insightful and forward-thinking.

Corresponding Formula:

Envision yourself as a [profession with particular strengths or insights]. Your task is to conceptualize [number] business ideas for [specific environment or condition]. Each idea should address [specific market need or trend] and highlight [business viability aspects]. Provide for each a brief [market analysis/starter strategy], leveraging [local resources/specific approaches]. Your writing should be [desired tone].

2. BUSINESS NAME:

Example No 1:

Prompt:

Assume the role of a seasoned brand executive, known for your expertise in developing successful branding strategies. Your task is to generate five distinct business names that are memorable, marketable, and relevant to a specific industry (please specify the industry). Each name should reflect innovation and appeal to the target demographic of that industry. Additionally, provide a brief rationale for each name, explaining how it aligns with brand identity and market trends. Write with a blend of creativity and strategic insight.

Corresponding Formula:

Assume the role of a [profession with specific expertise]. Your task is to generate [number] [type of creative output] that are [key characteristics required, e.g., memorable, marketable]. Each [output] should reflect [specific qualities] and appeal to [target demographic/industry, if applicable]. Additionally, provide a brief rationale for each, explaining how it aligns with [specific criteria, e.g., brand identity, market trends].

Write with a blend of [desired traits, e.g., creativity, strategic insight].

Example No 2:

Prompt:

Step into the shoes of an accomplished marketing guru with a knack for brand creation in the technology sector. Your challenge is to conceive five innovative business names that resonate with tech-savvy consumers and capture the essence of cutting-edge technology. Each name should be catchy, futuristic, and easy to remember. Alongside each name, provide a short explanation of how it connects with tech trends and consumer expectations in the technology market. Write in a style that is imaginative yet grounded in market realities.

Corresponding Formula:

Step into the shoes of a [profession with a specific skill or reputation] in the [specific sector]. Your challenge is to conceive [number] [type of creative output] that resonate with [target audience] and capture [desired theme or essence]. Each [output] should be [key characteristics, e.g., catchy, futuristic]. Alongside each, provide a short explanation of how it connects with [relevant trends and expectations]. Write in a style that is [desired traits, e.g., imaginative, realistic].

Example No 3:

Prompt:

Adopt the perspective of a veteran naming strategist specializing in the food and beverage industry. Devise five unique and appetizing business names that would appeal to food enthusiasts and reflect culinary innovation. Each name should evoke a sense of taste, quality, and originality. For each proposed name, include a brief description of how it conveys a unique aspect of the food and beverage experience, aligning with current gastronomic trends. Your approach should be creative yet mindful of industry nuances.

Corresponding Formula:

Adopt the perspective of a [profession with expertise] specializing in the [specific industry]. Devise [number] [type of creative output] that appeal to [target audience] and reflect [industry-specific theme]. Each [output] should evoke [key characteristics, e.g., sense of taste, quality]. For each, include a brief description of how it conveys [specific aspect of industry experience]. Your approach should be [desired traits, e.g., creative, industry-aware].

3. LOGO:

Example No 1:

Prompt:

Design a logo for my new business, '[insert business name from step 2]'. The business concept, as outlined in Step 1, is '[insert concept from Step 1]'. The logo should visually represent this concept and resonate with our target audience. It needs to be modern, distinctive, and scalable across various mediums. Please include a brief description of your design choices, explaining how each element of the logo aligns with our business concept and values. The design should be professional yet creative.

Corresponding Formula:

Design a [type of creative output] for [specified subject, e.g., my new business, project, etc.], '[insert relevant information]'. The [background or concept], as outlined in [previous step/reference], is '[insert relevant details]'. The [output] should [specific requirements, e.g., visually represent, resonate with audience]. It needs to be [key characteristics, e.g., modern, distinctive]. Please include a brief description of [your design choices], explaining how each element aligns with [relevant criteria, e.g., business concept, values]. The design should be [desired traits, e.g., professional, creative].

Example No 2:

Prompt:

Create a logo for my startup, '[insert business name from previous discussion]'. Our startup's core idea, '[insert core idea from earlier discussion]', should be the central theme of the logo. The design should be sleek, innovative, and appeal to a young, tech-savvy audience. It must also be adaptable for digital and print media. Include a concise explanation of how your design elements – color scheme, typography, and imagery – embody our startup's vision and appeal to our demographic. Aim for a balance between simplicity and creativity in your design.

Corresponding Formula:

Create a [type of creative output] for my [business/project], '[insert relevant information]'. The [core idea/theme], '[insert detail from earlier discussion]', should be central in the design. The design should be [desired characteristics, e.g., sleek, innovative]. It must also be adaptable for [specific mediums, e.g., digital, print]. Include a concise explanation of how [design elements] embody [specific criteria, e.g., startup's vision, target demographic]. Aim for a balance between [desired design traits, e.g., simplicity, creativity].

Example No 3:

Prompt:

Design a logo for my social enterprise, '[insert enterprise name from previous step]'. Reflect our mission, '[insert mission from previous step]', in the logo. The design should convey trustworthiness, community spirit, and sustainability. Ensure that it is visually impactful yet straightforward enough for easy recognition. Accompany the design with a brief rationale, detailing how it captures the essence of our social mission and is suitable for various communication channels. The style should be both professional and inviting.

Corresponding Formula:

Design a [type of creative output] for my [type of organization, e.g., social enterprise], '[insert relevant information]'. Reflect our [mission/core values], '[insert detail from previous step]', in the design. The design should convey [desired attributes, e.g., trustworthiness, sustainability]. Ensure it is [visual impact and recognition requirements]. Accompany the design with a brief rationale, detailing how it captures [specific criteria, e.g., social mission, communication adaptability]. The style should be both [desired style traits, e.g., professional, inviting].

4. OFFER:

Example No 1:

Prompt:

Utilizing Alex Hormozi's '$100m Offers' concept as a foundation, I would like to develop the core offer for our business. Please create a comprehensive and compelling core offer that aligns with our business model and target market. This offer should encapsulate the unique value proposition, pricing strategy, and customer benefits that distinguish our business in the market. Include key elements such as target audience, problem-solving approach, and potential guarantees or bonuses that make the offer irresistible. The development of this offer should be strategic, innovative, and directly aimed at driving significant business growth.

Corresponding Formula:

Utilizing [specific concept/framework], I would like to develop the [core business element] for our [type of business]. Please create a [adjectives describing the desired output, e.g., comprehensive, compelling] [output, e.g., core offer] that aligns with our [business model/target market]. This [output] should encapsulate the [key elements, e.g., unique value proposition, pricing strategy, customer benefits] that distinguish our business. Include [additional elements, e.g., target audience, problem-solving approach, guarantees/bonuses]. The development of this [output] should be [desired characteristics, e.g., strategic, innovative], aimed at [specific business goal, e.g., driving growth].

Example No 2:

Prompt:

Following the principles of Steve Blank's 'Lean Startup' methodology, I want to formulate the core offer for our new venture. Please craft a dynamic and scalable core offer that resonates with our lean startup approach and intended customer base. The offer should include elements of minimum viable product (MVP), customer feedback loops, and adaptability to market changes. Detail how this offer can attract early adopters and facilitate rapid iteration based on customer insights. The focus should be on efficiency, adaptability, and customer-centric design.

Corresponding Formula:

Following the principles of [notable entrepreneur's methodology], I want to formulate the [core business element] for our [type of business]. Please craft a [desired attributes, e.g., dynamic, scalable] [output, e.g., core offer] that resonates with our [specific approach/methodology] and [target audience]. The offer should include elements of [key methodology components, e.g., MVP, feedback loops, market adaptability]. Detail how this offer can [specific goals, e.g., attract early adopters, facilitate rapid iteration]. The focus should be on [key principles, e.g., efficiency, adaptability, customer-centric design].

Example No 3:

Prompt:

In line with Peter Thiel's 'Zero to One' concepts, let's develop our business's core offer. Please design an innovative and unique core offer that embodies the 'Zero to One' philosophy of creating something new and valuable. The offer should highlight how our business differentiates itself in a niche market, its monopoly potential, and its approach to solving a singular problem in a novel way. Explain how this offer will appeal to a market seeking groundbreaking solutions and establish us as a leader in the field. Emphasis should be on uniqueness, market disruption, and long-term vision.

Corresponding Formula:

In line with [notable entrepreneur's philosophy], let's develop the [core business element] for our [type of business]. Please design an [desired attributes, e.g., innovative, unique] [output, e.g., core offer] that embodies the [specific philosophy, e.g., 'Zero to One']. The offer should highlight [key aspects, e.g., differentiation in a niche market, monopoly potential, novel problem-solving approach]. Explain how this offer will [goals, e.g., appeal to a market seeking groundbreaking solutions, establish leadership]. Emphasis should be on [key principles, e.g., uniqueness, market disruption, long-term vision].

5. AUDIENCE:

Example No 1:

Prompt:

Assume the role of a marketing consultant tasked with identifying and defining our target audience. Our business is based in [location], and this should be considered in your analysis. Please develop a comprehensive audience segmentation, including a primary, secondary, and tertiary audience. For each audience tier, provide a detailed explanation of your reasoning, supported by data or market trends where possible. Include specific details such as demographics (age, gender, income), psychographics (interests, values, lifestyles), job titles, and geographical locations relevant to each audience. Your analysis should reflect a deep understanding of our market and how different audience segments interact with our product/service.

Corresponding Formula:

Assume the role of a [profession with a specific task, e.g., marketing consultant] tasked with [primary objective, e.g., identifying and defining our target audience]. Our business is based in [specific location], and this should be considered in your analysis. Please develop a [desired outcome, e.g., comprehensive audience segmentation], including a [list the types of segments, e.g., primary, secondary, tertiary audience]. For each [segment type], provide a detailed explanation of your reasoning, supported by [evidence type, e.g., data, market trends]. Include specific details such as [criteria to be included, e.g., demographics, psychographics, job titles, locations]. Your analysis should reflect [desired analytical depth, e.g., deep understanding of our market and audience interaction with our product/service].

Example No 2:

Prompt:

Step into the role of a digital marketing expert to help us pinpoint our online target audience. Our company is predominantly active in the digital space, with [insert specific industry or product details]. Your task is to segment our digital audience into primary, secondary, and tertiary groups. For each group, analyze and describe key characteristics, including online behavior patterns, preferred digital platforms, content preferences, and engagement tendencies. Also, consider factors such as age, location, digital literacy, and lifestyle. Explain how each group's attributes align with our digital marketing strategies and goals.

Corresponding Formula:

Step into the role of a [specific profession, e.g., digital marketing expert] to help us [specific task, e.g., pinpoint our online target audience]. Our company is [specific context, e.g., predominantly active in the digital space], with [insert specific industry or product details]. Your task is to [desired outcome, e.g., segment our digital audience] into [list segments, e.g., primary, secondary, tertiary groups]. For each group, analyze and describe [specific characteristics to analyze, e.g., online behavior patterns, platform preferences, engagement tendencies]. Also, consider [additional factors, e.g., age, location, digital literacy]. Explain how [each group's attributes] align with our [specific objectives, e.g., digital marketing strategies and goals].

Example No 3:

Prompt:

Take on the role of a brand strategist to assist in defining the target audience for our new product launch. We are a [location]-based company specializing in [product/service type]. You are tasked with creating a nuanced audience profile, identifying primary, secondary, and tertiary market segments. Focus on determining unique aspects such as buying motivations, lifestyle choices, income levels, and social influences that define each segment. Additionally, provide insights on geographical areas and cultural trends that may impact the appeal of our product/service. Your analysis should offer strategic guidance for our targeted marketing efforts.

Corresponding Formula:

Take on the role of a [specific profession, e.g., brand strategist] to assist in [specific task, e.g., defining the target audience for our new product launch]. We are a [location]-based company specializing in [product/service type]. You are tasked with creating a [desired outcome, e.g., nuanced audience profile], identifying [list segments, e.g., primary, secondary, tertiary market segments]. Focus on determining [unique aspects to analyze, e.g., buying motivations, lifestyle choices, income levels, social influences] for each segment. Additionally, provide insights on [factors like geographical areas and cultural trends]. Your analysis should offer [desired end goal, e.g., strategic guidance for our targeted marketing efforts].

6. COMPETITION:

Example No 1:

Prompt:

Assume the role of a specialized market researcher for our company, operating in the [insert industry] and located in [insert location]. Our core services include [insert services], and we primarily target [insert audience]. Your task is to conduct a thorough competitive analysis in [relevant locations]. Please categorize competitors into two lists:

1. *Direct Competitors: Identify 3-5 direct competitors. For each, provide the company name, URL, and a concise 2-3 sentence description of their services or products, highlighting how they directly compete with us.*
2. *Indirect Competitors: Identify 3-5 indirect competitors, explaining the reason for their classification as indirect. Include the same details as for direct competitors.*

If fewer than 3 competitors are found in either category, provide as many as possible. Following this, conduct a competitive analysis, summarizing key strategic insights such as market positioning, unique selling propositions, and any notable strengths or weaknesses. These insights should offer actionable recommendations for how we can enhance our business strategy.

Corresponding Formula:

Assume the role of a [profession, e.g., market researcher] for our company in the [industry] located in [location]. Our core services are [services], targeting [audience]. Your task is to [primary objective, e.g., conduct competitive analysis] in [relevant locations]. Categorize competitors into:

1. *Direct Competitors: [instructions for identifying direct competitors, including details to provide].*
2. *Indirect Competitors: [instructions for identifying indirect competitors, including details to provide].*

If fewer than [number] are found, provide as many as possible. Follow this with a [secondary objective, e.g., summarizing key strategic insights], offering [desired outcome, e.g., actionable recommendations for business strategy enhancement].

Example No 2:

Prompt:

Function as a strategic business analyst for our company in the [insert industry], based in [insert location]. We offer [insert services] and cater to [insert audience]. Your mission is to map out the competitive landscape in [relevant locations]. This should include:

1. *Primary Competitors: Identify and list 3-5 primary competitors. For each, provide the company name, website, and a brief description focusing on their core offerings and how they align or clash with our services.*
2. *Emerging Competitors: Identify 3-5 emerging or potential competitors, explaining their relevance despite being new or less established. Include the same details as for primary competitors.*

If the number of competitors in any category is less than 3, list as many as you can find. Conclude with a competitive analysis, highlighting market trends, potential threats, and opportunities, and suggest strategic actions we might consider to maintain or improve our market position.

Corresponding Formula:

Function as a [specific role, e.g., business analyst] for our company in the [industry], based in [location]. We offer [services] to [audience]. Your mission is to [task, e.g., map out the competitive landscape] in [locations]. This should include:

1. *Primary Competitors: [instructions for identifying primary competitors, including details to provide].*
2. *Emerging Competitors: [instructions for identifying emerging competitors, including details to provide].*

If the number is less than [number], list as many as you can find. Conclude with a [analysis objective, e.g., highlighting market trends, threats, and opportunities], and suggest [type of strategic actions].

Example No 3:

Prompt:

Work as a market intelligence expert for our [insert industry] company in [insert location], which specializes in [insert services] for [insert audience]. Your assignment involves a detailed competitor analysis in [relevant locations], broken down as follows:

1. *Market Leaders: Identify 3-5 market-leading competitors. Provide their company names, websites, and a short description that includes their market share, key products or services, and how they position themselves against companies like ours.*
2. *Niche Competitors: List 3-5 niche competitors, detailing why they are considered niche and their specific market segments. Include the same details as for market leaders.*

Should you find fewer than 3 in either category, include all available information. End with a comprehensive competitive analysis, focusing on areas such as innovation, customer loyalty, and branding strategies. Offer insights on how we can leverage these findings to strengthen our competitive edge.

Corresponding Formula:

Work as a [role, e.g., market intelligence expert] for our [industry] company in [location], specializing in [services] for [audience]. Your assignment involves [task, e.g., detailed competitor analysis] in [locations], broken down as follows:

1. *Market Leaders: [instructions for identifying market leaders, including details to provide].*
2. *Niche Competitors: [instructions for identifying niche competitors, including details to provide].*

Should you find fewer than [number], include all available information. End with a [analysis focus, e.g., focusing on innovation, customer loyalty, branding strategies], offering insights on [desired outcome, e.g., strengthening our competitive edge].

7. USP (UNIQUE SELLING PROPOSITION):

Example No 1:

Prompt:

Assume the role of an experienced marketing consultant for our business, which is currently facing challenges in defining a compelling UNIQUE SELLING PROPOSITION (USP). Our goal is to distinguish ourselves in a competitive market. Your task is to brainstorm and propose five innovative USP ideas that could significantly differentiate us from our competitors. Each idea should be unique, align with our brand values, and cater to our target audience's needs and preferences. For each proposed USP, include a brief explanation of how it can effectively set us apart and resonate with our customers, taking into account current market trends and consumer behaviors.

Corresponding Formula:

Assume the role of a [specific profession, e.g., marketing consultant] for our business, which is [current challenge, e.g., struggling with defining a UNIQUE SELLING PROPOSITION (USP)]. Our goal is to [desired outcome, e.g., distinguish ourselves in the market]. Your task is to [specific action required, e.g., brainstorm and propose USP ideas]. Propose [number] [type of ideas, e.g., innovative USP ideas] that [criteria for ideas, e.g., differentiate us from competitors, align with brand values]. For each [idea], include a brief explanation of how it [desired impact, e.g., sets us apart, resonates with customers], considering [relevant factors, e.g., market trends, consumer behaviors].

Example No 2:

Prompt:

Serve as a branding expert tasked with revitalizing our company's image. We are in the [insert industry] and currently facing challenges in distinguishing ourselves. We need you to conceptualize five powerful UNIQUE SELLING PROPOSITION (USP) ideas that could redefine our brand and make a lasting impression in the market. Each USP should be inventive, reflective of our core mission, and appealing to our primary demographic, [insert demographic details]. For each USP, provide a rationale as to how it can elevate our brand identity, appeal to consumer emotions, and capitalize on unmet needs or gaps in the market.

Corresponding Formula:

Serve as a [specific role, e.g., branding expert] tasked with [specific objective, e.g., revitalizing our company's image]. We are in the [industry] and currently facing [specific challenge]. We need you to [task, e.g., conceptualize UNIQUE SELLING PROPOSITION (USP) ideas]. Propose [number] [type of ideas, e.g., powerful USP ideas] that [desired qualities, e.g., redefine our brand, make a lasting impression]. Each USP should be [criteria, e.g., inventive, reflective of core mission, appealing to primary demographic]. For each USP, provide a rationale as to how it can [specific outcomes, e.g., elevate brand identity, appeal to emotions, capitalize on market gaps].

Example No 3:

Prompt:

Function as a strategic marketing consultant for our startup in the [insert industry]. We're seeking fresh perspectives to carve out a niche in a crowded market. Your assignment is to generate five distinctive UNIQUE SELLING PROPOSITION (USP) ideas that capture the essence of what makes our startup unique, especially focusing on [insert specific startup qualities or products]. Each idea should be groundbreaking, cater to trends in [insert industry], and address the evolving preferences of our target audience. Alongside each USP, explain its potential to disrupt the market and create a strong brand connection.

Corresponding Formula:

Function as a [role, e.g., strategic marketing consultant] for our startup in the [industry]. We're seeking [objective, e.g., fresh perspectives for a niche]. Your assignment is to [task, e.g., generate distinctive USP ideas]. Propose [number] [type of ideas, e.g., distinctive USP ideas] that [desired attributes, e.g., capture the essence of our startup, focus on specific qualities]. Each idea should be [criteria, e.g., groundbreaking, cater to industry trends, address audience preferences]. Alongside each USP, explain its [potential outcomes, e.g., market disruption capability, brand connection strength].

8. VALUE PROPOSITION:

Example No 1:

Prompt:

Adopt the role of a business strategist, using Alex Osterwalder's Value Proposition Canvas as a guiding framework. Our objective is to develop a compelling value proposition for our company. Please analyze our customer segments and their needs, pains, and gains as outlined in Osterwalder's model. Then, craft a strong value proposition that directly addresses these aspects, linking our products/services to the customer's desires and challenges. The value proposition should be concise, clearly articulate the benefits of our offerings, and demonstrate how we uniquely solve our customers' problems or enhance their success. Include a brief explanation of how each element of the value proposition aligns with the customer segments identified.

Corresponding Formula:

Adopt the role of a [profession, e.g., business strategist], using [specific framework, e.g., Alex Osterwalder's Value Proposition Canvas] as a guiding framework. Our objective is to [specific task, e.g., develop a compelling value proposition] for our company. Analyze our [customer segments and their characteristics]. Then, craft a [desired quality, e.g., strong] value proposition that [desired outcome, e.g., addresses customer needs, pains, and gains]. The value proposition should be [specific characteristics, e.g., concise, clear, benefit-oriented] and demonstrate how we [solve problems/enhance success]. Include a brief explanation of how each element aligns with the [identified customer segments].

Example No 2:

Prompt:

Assume the role of a marketing specialist, applying Simon Sinek's 'Start With Why' approach to formulating our value proposition. We aim to establish a value proposition that deeply resonates with our audience's beliefs and motivations. Begin by identifying the core 'why' behind our business — our fundamental purpose, cause, or belief that inspires what we do. Then, develop a value proposition that communicates this 'why' clearly, linking it to the benefits of our products/services. The proposition should not only describe what we offer but also why it matters, emphasizing how it aligns with the values and aspirations of our target audience.

Corresponding Formula:

Assume the role of a [role, e.g., marketing specialist], applying [methodology, e.g., Simon Sinek's 'Start With Why'] to [task, e.g., formulating our value proposition]. Begin by [initial step, e.g., identifying the core 'why' behind our business]. Then, develop a [desired outcome, e.g., value proposition] that [specific goals, e.g., communicates the 'why', links benefits]. The proposition should [requirements, e.g., describe offerings, emphasize alignment with audience values].

Example No 3:

Prompt:

Work as a strategic consultant using Clayton Christensen's 'Jobs to be Done' theory to create our value proposition. Focus on understanding the main 'jobs' our customers need to accomplish and how our products/services can fulfill these jobs effectively. Analyze our target market to determine the specific tasks, challenges, or desires our customers face. Craft a value proposition that articulates how our solutions are uniquely suited to 'do the job' for our customers, enhancing their lives or solving their problems. This proposition should clearly depict the practicality and uniqueness of our offerings in meeting customer needs.

Corresponding Formula:

Work as a [role, e.g., strategic consultant] using [theory, e.g., Clayton Christensen's 'Jobs to be Done'] to [task, e.g., create our value proposition]. Focus on [initial step, e.g., understanding the main 'jobs' customers need]. Analyze [target market characteristics]. Craft a [desired outcome, e.g., value proposition] that [specific goals, e.g., articulates how solutions fulfill jobs]. The proposition should [requirements, e.g., depict practicality, uniqueness in meeting customer needs].

9. MARKETING CHANNELS:

Example No 1:

Prompt:

Act as a marketing strategy expert for [company name]. Our goal is to identify the most effective marketing channels for our business. Please conduct a comprehensive analysis of potential marketing channels, considering our industry, target audience, and product/service offerings. For each recommended channel, provide a detailed rationale, including factors such as audience reach, engagement potential, cost-effectiveness, and alignment with our brand's messaging and goals. Additionally, consider the integration of digital and traditional channels and how they can synergistically work to maximize our marketing impact. Your analysis should offer strategic insights to guide our decision-making process in selecting the optimal marketing mix.

Corresponding Formula:

Act as a [profession, e.g., marketing strategy expert] for [company name]. Our goal is to [task, e.g., identify effective marketing channels]. Conduct a [analysis type, e.g., comprehensive analysis] of [potential marketing channels], considering [relevant factors, e.g., industry, target audience, product/service offerings]. For each [recommended channel], provide a [details of analysis, e.g., detailed rationale including factors such as audience reach, engagement potential]. Additionally, consider [additional aspects, e.g., integration of digital and traditional channels]. Your analysis should offer [desired outcome, e.g., strategic insights to guide decision-making in selecting marketing mix].

Example No 2:

Prompt:

Function as a digital marketing consultant for [company name], which specializes in [insert industry/product/service]. Your mission is to evaluate and recommend digital marketing channels most suitable for our brand. Analyze various online channels, including social media platforms, search engines, email marketing, and influencer partnerships. For each channel you suggest, provide a comprehensive justification based on factors like target audience alignment, digital trends, cost efficiency, and potential ROI. Also, assess how each channel can be optimized for our specific marketing goals and brand voice, ensuring a cohesive and effective online presence.

Corresponding Formula:

Function as a [role, e.g., digital marketing consultant] for [company name], specializing in [industry/product/service]. Your mission is to [task, e.g., evaluate and recommend digital marketing channels]. Analyze [specific channels, e.g., social media, search engines, email marketing]. For each [suggested channel], provide a [type of justification, e.g., comprehensive justification] based on factors like [criteria, e.g., audience alignment, digital trends, cost efficiency]. Also, assess how each [channel] can be optimized for [specific goals, e.g., marketing goals, brand voice], ensuring [desired outcome, e.g., cohesive online presence].

Example No 3:

Prompt:

Assume the role of an integrated marketing strategist for [company name], a business in the [insert industry]. We need a strategic evaluation of both digital and traditional marketing channels that align with our brand and market position. Investigate and list relevant channels like TV, radio, print, online advertising, social media, and content marketing. For each proposed channel, analyze its effectiveness in reaching our target audience, enhancing brand awareness, and driving customer engagement. Discuss the cost-benefit ratio, potential reach, and integration possibilities with other marketing efforts. Your insights should help us craft a balanced and effective overall marketing strategy.

Corresponding Formula:

Assume the role of an [role, e.g., integrated marketing strategist] for [company name], in the [industry]. We need [task, e.g., strategic evaluation of marketing channels]. Investigate and list [channels, e.g., TV, radio, print, online]. For each [proposed channel], analyze its [effectiveness criteria, e.g., audience reach, brand awareness, customer engagement]. Discuss the [analysis aspects, e.g., cost-benefit ratio, potential reach, integration with other efforts]. Your insights should [desired outcome, e.g., help craft a balanced marketing strategy].

10. COLOUR SCHEME:

Example No 1:

Prompt:

Step into the role of an experienced graphic designer and artist for our brand. Our objective is to develop an attention-grabbing and brand-appropriate color scheme for our artwork. Please create a color scheme that reflects our brand identity and resonates with our target audience. Provide hex codes for each color you select, along with a detailed explanation of why each color was chosen, how they complement each other, and the emotions or messages they convey. Also, specify the contexts or applications (e.g., digital media, print, product design) where each color should be primarily used, considering visibility and aesthetic coherence.

Corresponding Formula:

Step into the role of a [specific profession, e.g., graphic designer and artist] for our brand. Our objective is to [task, e.g., develop an attention-grabbing color scheme]. Please create a [outcome, e.g., color scheme] that [criteria, e.g., reflects brand identity, resonates with target audience]. Provide [specific elements, e.g., hex codes for each color], along with a [type of explanation, e.g., detailed explanation] of [reasons for choices, e.g., why each color was chosen, emotional/message conveyance]. Also, specify [applications, e.g., contexts or applications for each color], considering [relevant factors, e.g., visibility, aesthetic coherence].

Example No 2:

Prompt:

Assume the role of a creative brand designer for our company, which operates in the [insert industry]. We are looking to revitalize our visual identity with a fresh and modern color scheme. Your task is to design a palette that is both innovative and reflective of current industry trends. Provide hex codes for the selected colors, and offer an explanation for each choice based on color psychology, market trends, and how they align with our brand values. Additionally, suggest how these colors can be effectively used across various platforms, such as our website, marketing materials, and product packaging, to ensure brand consistency.

Corresponding Formula:

> *Assume the role of a [profession, e.g., creative brand designer] for our company in the [industry]. Your task is to [objective, e.g., design a fresh and modern color palette]. Provide [requirements, e.g., hex codes for selected colors], and offer an explanation for each based on [criteria, e.g., color psychology, market trends, brand alignment]. Additionally, suggest how these colors can be [application, e.g., used across various platforms] to [desired outcome, e.g., ensure brand consistency].*

Example No 3:

Prompt:

> *Work as a freelance graphic artist collaborating with our [insert business type] business. We aim to create a distinctive color scheme that stands out in our niche market. Develop a color palette that captures the unique essence of our brand, considering our unconventional approach and target demographic. Provide hex codes for each color, and describe how each contributes to creating a compelling visual story for our brand. Explain how the colors can enhance customer engagement, particularly in digital content and social media presence, where visual impact is crucial.*

Corresponding Formula:

> *Work as a [profession, e.g., freelance graphic artist] collaborating with our [business type]. Your aim is to [task, e.g., create a distinctive color scheme for the niche market]. Develop a [outcome, e.g., color palette] that captures [brand essence, e.g., unique essence of our brand]. Provide [requirements, e.g., hex codes for each color], and describe how each [contributes to, e.g., creates a compelling visual story]. Explain how the colors can [application, e.g., enhance customer engagement] particularly in [specific areas, e.g., digital content, social media].*

11. TONE OF VOICE:

Example No 1:

Prompt:

> *Take on the role of an expert copywriter to develop a detailed brand tone of voice and style guide for our company. This guide should comprehensively cover the following aspects:*
>
> 1. *Precise Tone of Voice: Define a specific tone of voice that aligns with our brand identity and target audience. Provide a clear explanation for this choice, detailing how it reflects our brand values and resonates with our audience.*
> 2. *Word Usage: List words and phrases that should be used or avoided in our branding and marketing materials. Explain how these choices support our brand tone and messaging strategy.*
> 3. *Key Messaging Ideas: Suggest key messaging themes or ideas that align with our brand's goals and values, enhancing our communication effectiveness.*

4. *Punctuation and Grammar Guidelines: Establish guidelines for punctuation and grammar that support the brand tone and ensure clarity and consistency in all communications.*

Please present the guide in a clear and structured format, preferably using markup for easy reference and implementation.

Corresponding Formula:

Take on the role of a [specific profession, e.g., expert copywriter] to develop a [document type, e.g., brand tone of voice and style guide] for our company. The guide should cover:

1. *[Specific aspect, e.g., Precise Tone of Voice]: Define a [desired characteristic, e.g., specific tone] that aligns with [brand identity, target audience]. Provide an explanation for [choice, relevance].*
2. *[Specific aspect, e.g., Word Usage]: List [words/phrases to use/avoid]. Explain how these [support brand tone, messaging strategy].*
3. *[Specific aspect, e.g., Key Messaging Ideas]: Suggest [themes/ideas] that align with [brand goals, values].*
4. *[Specific aspect, e.g., Punctuation and Grammar Guidelines]: Establish [guidelines] that support [brand tone, communication clarity].*

Present the guide in [desired format, e.g., clear, structured format using markup].

Example No 2:

Prompt:

Function as a branding specialist and develop a comprehensive brand language guide for our [insert company type]. The guide should encompass the following elements:

1. *Brand Voice Characterization: Establish a distinct brand voice that captures our unique identity and ethos. Describe its characteristics (e.g., professional, friendly, authoritative) and justify why this voice aligns with our brand personality and audience expectations.*
2. *Vocabulary and Phraseology: Curate a list of specific terms, phrases, and language styles that embody our brand voice. Clarify which terms should be emphasized for brand consistency and which ones to avoid to maintain our brand integrity.*
3. *Communication Themes: Outline several core themes or narratives that should be central to our messaging across all platforms, reflecting our brand's core values and mission.*
4. *Style and Formatting Norms: Define clear guidelines for style, formatting, and grammar that enhance readability and convey our brand voice coherently.*

Present this guide in a user-friendly format, with annotations or markup for practical application by our content team.

Corresponding Formula:

Function as a [role, e.g., branding specialist] and develop a [document type, e.g., brand language guide] for our [company type]. The guide should encompass:

1. *[Aspect, e.g., Brand Voice Characterization]: Establish [voice characteristics] and justify [alignment with brand and audience].*
2. *[Aspect, e.g., Vocabulary and Phraseology]: Curate [specific terms and styles], clarify [terms to emphasize or avoid].*
3. *[Aspect, e.g., Communication Themes]: Outline [core themes/narratives] reflecting [brand values and mission].*
4. *[Aspect, e.g., Style and Formatting Norms]: Define [guidelines for style, formatting, grammar].*

Present in a [format, e.g., user-friendly format with annotations/markup].

Example No 3:

Prompt:

As a skilled content strategist, create a bespoke tone of voice and writing style manual for our [insert company type] brand. This manual should detail:

1. *Brand Voice Definition: Craft a unique voice that embodies our brand's character, discussing its tone, mood, and level of formality. Explain the rationale behind the chosen voice, considering our market positioning and customer demographics.*
2. *Linguistic Guidelines: Offer specific guidelines on language use, including dos and don'ts in terms of word choice, sentence structure, and brand-specific jargon, to maintain a cohesive brand narrative.*
3. *Messaging Pillars: Identify key messaging pillars that should consistently resonate in our content, aligning with our strategic objectives and brand promise.*
4. *Editorial Standards: Set comprehensive standards for grammar, punctuation, and overall writing style that uphold our brand's quality and clarity standards.*

Ensure the manual is structured for clarity and ease of use, with examples illustrating each guideline for our editorial team.

Corresponding Formula:

As a [role, e.g., content strategist], create a [document type, e.g., tone of voice and writing style manual] for our [company type] brand. This manual should detail:

1. *[Aspect, e.g., Brand Voice Definition]: Craft [voice characteristics], explain [rationale considering market position, customer demographics].*
2. *[Aspect, e.g., Linguistic Guidelines]: Offer [guidelines on language use], including [dos and don'ts in word choice, structure, jargon].*
3. *[Aspect, e.g., Messaging Pillars]: Identify [key messaging pillars] aligning with [strategic objectives, brand promise].*
4. *[Aspect, e.g., Editorial Standards]: Set [standards for grammar, punctuation,*

style].

Ensure the manual is [format, e.g., structured for clarity and ease of use], with [examples illustrating guidelines].

12. CONTENT IDEAS:

<u>Example No 1:</u>

Prompt:

As a content strategist, now that we have established our marketing channels, tone of voice, and color scheme, we require your expertise to brainstorm core themes for our marketing content. Please develop 10 overarching themes that align with our brand's messaging and marketing objectives. For each theme, create 5 relevant subtopics. Under each subtopic, propose 3 specific content ideas. For each content idea, provide the following details:

1. *Idea/Topic: Clearly define the subject or focus of the content.*
2. *Format: Specify the content format (e.g., blog post, video, infographic).*
3. *Channel: Indicate the most suitable marketing channel for each content idea (e.g., social media, website, email).*

This structured approach will guide our content creation efforts, ensuring consistency and alignment with our brand strategy.

Corresponding Formula:

As a [profession, e.g., content strategist], with established [brand elements, e.g., marketing channels, tone, color scheme], you are required to [task, e.g., brainstorm core themes for marketing content]. Develop [number] [output, e.g., overarching themes] that align with [criteria, e.g., brand's messaging, marketing objectives]. For each theme, create [number] [sub-output, e.g., relevant subtopics]. Under each subtopic, propose [number] [specific content ideas]. For each content idea, provide:

1. *[Element, e.g., Idea/Topic]: [Description requirement, e.g., define the subject/focus].*
2. *[Element, e.g., Format]: [Specification, e.g., specify content format].*
3. *[Element, e.g., Channel]: [Indication, e.g., indicate suitable marketing channel].*

This approach will [desired outcome, e.g., guide content creation, ensure brand consistency].

<u>Example No 2:</u>

Prompt:

As a creative marketing specialist, with our defined marketing channels, brand tone, and color scheme in mind, your next task is to conceptualize distinct content pillars for our marketing strategy. We need you to outline 10 primary content pillars that embody our brand ethos and marketing goals. Under each pillar, identify 4 key topics that represent the pillar's theme. For each topic, generate 2 unique content ideas, including:

1. Idea/Concept: Detail the core concept or angle of the content.
2. Preferred Format: Suggest the ideal format for presenting this idea (e.g., podcast episode, interactive web content).
3. Recommended Channel: Recommend the best channel for each idea based on its nature and our audience's preferences (e.g., LinkedIn, YouTube, blog).

This will form the backbone of our content marketing strategy, ensuring thematic consistency and audience engagement.

Corresponding Formula:

As a [profession, e.g., creative marketing specialist], with [established elements, e.g., marketing channels, brand tone, color scheme], your task is to [objective, e.g., conceptualize content pillars]. Outline [number] [output, e.g., primary content pillars] embodying [brand and marketing criteria, e.g., brand ethos, marketing goals]. Under each pillar, identify [number] [sub-output, e.g., key topics]. For each topic, generate [number] [content ideas], including:

1. [Element, e.g., Idea/Concept]: [Detail requirements, e.g., detail core concept/angle].
2. [Element, e.g., Preferred Format]: [Suggestion requirement, e.g., suggest ideal format].
3. [Element, e.g., Recommended Channel]: [Recommendation requirement, e.g., recommend best channel].

This will [desired outcome, e.g., form the backbone of content marketing strategy, ensure engagement].

Example No 3:

Prompt:

In your role as a digital content planner, and in line with our existing marketing framework, we require you to establish comprehensive content themes for our digital marketing efforts. Develop 8 overarching content themes that resonate with our digital strategy and brand narrative. For each theme, propose 3 major subtopics that explore different aspects of the theme. Beneath each subtopic, brainstorm 3 specific content pieces, which should include:

1. Topic Focus: Clearly articulate the main idea or theme of the content.
2. Content Type: Determine the most effective type of content for the topic (e.g., short-form video, blog series).
3. Optimal Digital Platform: Identify which digital platform (e.g., Instagram, company website, email newsletter) best suits each content piece, based on our

audience demographics and platform strengths.

This structure will help streamline our digital content creation, enhancing brand presence and audience relevance.

Corresponding Formula:

In your role as a [profession, e.g., digital content planner], with our [established marketing framework], your task is to [objective, e.g., establish content themes for digital marketing]. Develop [number] [output, e.g., overarching content themes] resonating with [digital strategy, brand narrative]. For each theme, propose [number] [sub-output, e.g., major subtopics]. Beneath each subtopic, brainstorm [number] [specific content pieces], which should include:

1. *[Element, e.g., Topic Focus]: [Articulation requirement, e.g., clearly articulate main idea/theme].*
2. *[Element, e.g., Content Type]: [Determination requirement, e.g., determine most effective content type].*
3. *[Element, e.g., Optimal Digital Platform]: [Identification requirement, e.g., identify best digital platform].*

This structure will [desired outcome, e.g., streamline digital content creation, enhance brand presence].

13. CONTENT CALENDAR:

Example No 1:

Prompt:

As a content management specialist, now that we have our content ideas, we require you to create an organized content calendar starting from [date]. This calendar should be presented in a table format and include the following details for each content piece:

1. *Posting Date: Specify the exact date for publishing each piece of content.*
2. *Posting Time: If applicable, provide the specific time for posting, considering optimal engagement times for each channel.*
3. *Posting Channel: Indicate the channel (e.g., social media platform, blog, newsletter) where each content piece will be published.*
4. *Repurposing Opportunities: Identify potential ways to repurpose or upcycle each content piece across different platforms or formats to maximize reach and engagement.*

Ensure that the calendar is clear, detailed, and structured to facilitate easy implementation and tracking of our content strategy.

Corresponding Formula:

As a [profession, e.g., content management specialist], with [established content ideas], you are required to [task, e.g., create an organized content calendar] starting from [specified date]. The calendar should be in [format, e.g., table format] and include:

1. *[Element, e.g., Posting Date]: [Detail, e.g., specify exact date for each content piece].*
2. *[Element, e.g., Posting Time]: [Detail, e.g., provide specific time, considering engagement times].*
3. *[Element, e.g., Posting Channel]: [Indicate, e.g., indicate the channel for each content piece].*
4. *[Element, e.g., Repurposing Opportunities]: [Identify, e.g., identify ways to repurpose content across platforms/formats].*

Ensure the calendar is [qualities, e.g., clear, detailed, structured] for [desired outcome, e.g., easy implementation and tracking of content strategy].

Example No 2:

Prompt:

Assuming the role of a digital marketing coordinator, use our finalized list of content ideas to construct a comprehensive content schedule starting from [date]. Present this schedule in a spreadsheet format, including the following elements for each content item:

1. *Release Date: Specify the date for each content item's release.*
2. *Optimal Posting Time: If relevant, determine the best time for posting to maximize audience engagement, based on analytics data.*
3. *Distribution Platform: Indicate which digital platform (e.g., Facebook, Twitter, company blog) each content item will be shared on.*
4. *Cross-Posting Strategies: For each content piece, suggest potential cross-posting or content recycling strategies on other platforms or formats, enhancing content visibility and lifespan.*

Your content schedule should be easy to follow, aiding in the effective and timely deployment of our digital marketing strategy.

Corresponding Formula:

Assuming the role of a [profession, e.g., digital marketing coordinator], use [content ideas] to construct a [document type, e.g., comprehensive content schedule] starting from [date]. Present in [format, e.g., spreadsheet format], including:

1. *[Element, e.g., Release Date]: [Specify release dates for each content item].*
2. *[Element, e.g., Optimal Posting Time]: [Determine best posting times based on analytics data].*
3. *[Element, e.g., Distribution Platform]: [Indicate the digital platform for each content item].*
4. *[Element, e.g., Cross-Posting Strategies]: [Suggest cross-posting/recycling*

strategies].

Ensure the schedule is [qualities, e.g., easy to follow], aiding in [desired outcome, e.g., effective deployment of digital marketing strategy].

Example No 3:

Prompt:

As a content planning expert, you are tasked with creating a detailed editorial calendar for our upcoming content, starting from [date]. This calendar should be organized in a visual planner or calendar tool, and should outline:

1. *Publishing Schedule: Mark the specific dates on which each content piece should be published.*
2. *Timing for Release: Note the ideal times for release for each content type, considering peak user activity times.*
3. *Content Distribution Channels: Clearly indicate where each content piece will be published or shared, such as specific social media platforms, email newsletters, or our website.*
4. *Content Adaptation Opportunities: Identify possibilities for adapting each content piece for different mediums or subsequent postings, to extend its reach and efficacy.*

This calendar should serve as a clear, actionable guide for our entire marketing team, facilitating a coordinated and consistent content rollout.

Corresponding Formula:

As a [profession, e.g., content planning expert], you are tasked with creating a [document type, e.g., detailed editorial calendar] starting from [date]. Organize in [format, e.g., visual planner or calendar tool], outlining:

1. *[Element, e.g., Publishing Schedule]: [Mark specific dates for publishing each content piece].*
2. *[Element, e.g., Timing for Release]: [Note ideal release times, considering user activity].*
3. *[Element, e.g., Content Distribution Channels]: [Indicate where each content piece will be published].*
4. *[Element, e.g., Content Adaptation Opportunities]: [Identify adaptation possibilities for different mediums].*

Ensure the calendar serves as a [qualities, e.g., clear, actionable guide] for [desired outcome, e.g., coordinated content rollout].

Chapter 20
LIMITATIONS

While ChatGPT shows remarkable capabilities in generating human-like text, it's crucial to understand its inherent limitations. Recognizing these constraints can help you set realistic expectations and use the tool more effectively.

- **Data Cut-off and Real-time Information:** As of my last update in April 2023, ChatGPT's knowledge base is static and does not include events or developments occurring after its last training cut-off. It cannot provide insights on or react to current happenings or trends emerging post-cut-off.
- **Contextual Memory Limit:** GPT-4 significantly enhances contextual memory capacity, accommodating up to 32,000 tokens, roughly equating to 25,000 words or approximately 50 pages of text. This expanded memory allows for the processing and summarization of extensive documents, facilitating detailed discussions within a single session.
- **Output Limitation:** ChatGPT enforces an output limit to balance computational resources and response quality. While GPT-4 can generate responses up to approximately 3,000 words, complex inquiries may prematurely reach this threshold. If the response is truncated, you can prompt the model to "Continue" in order to help resume the narrative. For best results, segment intricate queries into manageable parts for sequential submission.
- **Literal Interpretation and Figurative Language:** The model's literal nature means it may misinterpret sarcasm, irony, and other forms of figurative language, potentially leading to inaccurate or nonsensical responses.
- **Bias and Fairness:** Reflecting the biases present in its training data, ChatGPT's outputs can sometimes perpetuate these biases. Continuous efforts are made to mitigate bias and ensure fairness, but it's an ongoing challenge in AI.
- **Privacy Considerations:** ChatGPT does not keep personal information across sessions; however, it processes input data within a session to generate responses. You should be mindful of privacy implications and review OpenAI's privacy policy before sharing sensitive information.
- **Improvements and Future Capabilities:** The landscape of AI and machine learning evolves rapidly, with OpenAI committed to enhancing ChatGPT's functionalities, including potential real-time information updates and bias mitigation strategies. We encourage you to stay informed about updates and advancements.
- **Due Diligence:** Given these limitations, exercise due diligence and critical judgment when using ChatGPT's outputs, especially for decision-making or content creation purposes.

Chapter 21
CONCLUSIONS

As we reach the culmination of our exploration into harnessing ChatGPT for unparalleled financial achievement, it's clear that the journey we've embarked on is both revolutionary and expansive. From igniting new business ventures to amplifying the growth of established enterprises and empowering freelancers with superhuman capabilities, ChatGPT stands as a beacon of innovation and efficiency.

Our dive into diverse prompt examples and best practices for prompting has unveiled the vast potential of ChatGPT to craft content that resonates deeply with audiences, streamline workflows, and foster creative repurposing across digital platforms. The path from ideation to monetization—spanning YouTube channels, E-books, courses, and blogs—has been demystified, showcasing ChatGPT as an indispensable ally in content creation and digital marketing.

The essence of our journey reveals that while ChatGPT is a formidable tool in the quest for financial success, the underlying force propelling you towards the coveted million-dollar milestone is the fusion of innovative technology with human ingenuity, perseverance, and strategic foresight. Embracing ChatGPT not merely as a tool but as a companion in your entrepreneurial endeavors amplifies your capacity to navigate the complexities of modern business landscapes with agility and vision.

Echoing the wisdom of Steve Jobs, let ChatGPT transcend its role as a tool to become a companion on your path to success. We designed this book as a blueprint for those who dare to innovate and adapt in pursuit of financial aspirations. It is fortified with prompts, strategies, and insights of broad applicability. Yet, the journey to your first million underscores a timeless truth: success is a testament to hard work, strategic planning, and an unwavering commitment to your vision.

May this book serve not only as a guide but as a source of inspiration, driving you to explore new horizons, overcome challenges, and seize the opportunities that lie at the intersection of artificial intelligence and entrepreneurial spirit. With ChatGPT by your side, the pursuit of financial independence is not just a possibility but a tangible goal within your reach.

Chapter 22
SHARE THE WEALTH

Would you consider extending a gesture of generosity that costs nothing yet could change lives? In just a moment of your time, you can make a difference.

Imagine, at this very instant, there's someone out there eager to unlock the secrets of financial independence, dreaming of turning their visions into reality, and navigating the complexities of entrepreneurship. They are in search of the same insightful guidance that this book aims to provide.

Your insights through a review can act as a lighthouse for countless aspiring entrepreneurs:

- Illuminate the path to financial freedom for someone on the brink of discovery.
- Empower individuals to elevate their lives and those of their loved ones.
- Provide the pivotal advice that turns aspiration into achievement.
- Spark a positive transformation in the entrepreneurial journey of others.

By sharing your experience with this book, you contribute to the entrepreneurial success stories of tomorrow. And if you find the strategies within these pages transformative, why not spread the word? A recommendation from you can be the pivotal moment someone recalls as the start of their success story.

From the bottom of our hearts, we extend our deepest gratitude for your role in fostering a community of growth, innovation, and shared success.

Please scan this QR code to leave your kind, positive review.

Wishing you all the best,

Mauricio

Appendix No 1
The Simple Guide to Wealth *(BONUS No 1)*

This guide offers actionable insights and methodologies for achieving financial independence. It breaks down complex financial concepts into practical steps, covering everything from establishing an emergency fund, overcoming debt, to strategic investment and risk management.

Aimed at empowering you with the knowledge necessary for informed financial decision-making, it emphasizes the importance of a proactive approach to saving, investing, and budgeting. By integrating psychological aspects, this guide equips you with a holistic strategy for wealth building and financial well-being, making the journey towards financial freedom both achievable and sustainable.

To have access to this guide, please scan this QR code. Before reading this guide, please read its disclaimer:

Appendix No 2
Prompts *(BONUS No 2)*

There are over 500 prompts, crafted to enhance conversations with ChatGPT across diverse subjects such as business, career advancement, ChatGPt learning, copywriting, creativity, entrepreneurship, marketing, productivity, sales, side hustle ideas, social media, and more. Each prompt is accompanied by a unique formula, allowing for customization to your specific needs and scenarios, and is further supported by hundreds of examples to illustrate versatile applications.

This collection caters to a wide range of conversational objectives, from generating creative content to making smarter decisions, and is categorized into specialized themes for targeted engagement.

We encourage you to further adapt and refine the prompts and formulas to your business and projects to ensure relevance and depth in interactions with ChatGPT. Whether for professional development, learning, or creative exploration, these prompts equip you with the tools to navigate and leverage AI conversations effectively, fostering enhanced understanding, innovation, and strategic insight.

To have access to the prompts, formulas, and examples, please scan this QR code:

Appendix No 3
Follow-up Prompts *(BONUS No 3)*

There are 1100 generic prompts that you can use as follow-ups in order to get more specific or revised information from ChatGPT. Don't forget to tailor these prompts to your specific circumstances and to the response you previously received from the Chatbot.

Each of these prompt types serves a different purpose and can be used effectively in different scenarios. Depending on the context and the intended outcome, one type of prompt may be more suitable than another.

These prompts are divided into eleven distinct categories, each tailored to specific conversational needs: Generic, Enhancement, Clarification, Probing, Critical Thinking, Instructional, Exploration, Comparison, Summarization, Evaluation, and Hypothetical.

To have access to the follow-up prompts, please scan this QR code:

Appendix No 4
Business and Entrepreneurial Professionals

This list is tailored to professions who help to drive success, innovation, and growth in entrepreneurial and business settings. They play crucial roles in guiding entrepreneurs and business owners towards achieving substantial financial success and realizing their business objectives. To maximize the utility of this list, we recommend employing the 'Act as' best practice to get their insights and wisdom.

1. Business Mentor: Offers insights and guidance to entrepreneurs for both start-up success and sustained business growth.
2. Entrepreneurial Coach: Specializes in assisting entrepreneurs in developing business strategies, market positioning, and operational efficiency.
3. Business Leader: Influences and directs business teams towards achieving aggressive financial targets and company-wide objectives.
4. Start-up Consultant: Provides expertise in launching successful start-ups, focusing on innovation, funding strategies, and market entry.
5. Growth Strategist: Aids businesses in scaling operations, expanding market reach, and accelerating revenue growth.
6. Financial Advisor for Entrepreneurs: Guides business owners in financial planning, investment strategies, and capital management for business expansion.
7. Business Development Consultant: Focuses on identifying growth opportunities, strategic partnerships, and new market entry for businesses.

8. Sales Optimization Coach: Enhances sales strategies, team performance, and overall sales effectiveness for revenue growth.
9. Marketing and Branding Expert: Advises on creating impactful marketing strategies and building a strong brand presence in competitive markets.
10. Product Development Specialist: Guides the process of product ideation, development, and launch to ensure market fit and profitability.
11. E-commerce Specialist: Provides strategies for successful online business operations, digital marketing, and customer acquisition.
12. Investment and Funding Advisor: Offers insights on securing funding, managing investments, and financial strategies for business expansion.
13. Operational Efficiency Expert: Focuses on streamlining business operations to increase productivity and reduce costs.
14. Customer Experience Strategist: Enhances customer engagement, satisfaction, and loyalty strategies to drive sales and brand advocacy.
15. Technology Integration Consultant: Advises on incorporating technology to optimize business operations and drive innovation.
16. Digital Transformation Coach: Guides businesses in adopting digital practices to stay competitive and relevant in the market.
17. Supply Chain Optimization Expert: Enhances supply chain processes for efficiency, cost reduction, and improved profitability.
18. Risk Management Consultant: Advises on identifying, assessing, and mitigating business risks to protect financial interests.
19. Global Expansion Strategist: Provides insights on international market entry, global operations, and cross-border business strategies.
20. Sustainability Advisor for Businesses: Focuses on integrating sustainable practices for long-term business success and social responsibility.
21. Franchise Development Expert: Guides in expanding business through franchising, franchise management, and growth strategies.
22. Mergers and Acquisitions Specialist: Advises on business acquisition strategies, merger processes, and integration for growth.
23. Corporate Restructuring Consultant: Assists in restructuring business operations for efficiency, profitability, and market adaptability.
24. Innovation and Creativity Coach: Encourages creative thinking and innovation to develop unique business solutions and products.
25. Entrepreneurship Advisor: Offers comprehensive guidance on starting, managing, and growing a profitable business.

Appendix No 5
Tones for Business and Entrepreneurial Success

The tone of communication significantly influences business and entrepreneurial interactions. The right tone can foster trust, drive motivation, and facilitate effective communication, aligning with the goal of achieving significant financial success.

1. Motivational: Inspires action and a positive approach towards achieving substantial business milestones.

2. Strategic: Demonstrates a calculated and planned approach to business decisions and actions.
3. Authoritative: Exudes confidence and expertise, essential in guiding teams and making decisive business choices.
4. Innovative: Encourages thinking outside the box, crucial for business growth and standing out in the market.
5. Supportive: Offers encouragement and backup, especially during entrepreneurial challenges and risks.
6. Analytical: Applies critical and logical analysis to business situations, aiding in informed decision-making.
7. Advisory: Provides expert suggestions based on in-depth business knowledge and market understanding.
8. Assertive: Encourages clear, confident communication of business needs and goals.
9. Respectful: Maintains a professional respect for partners, clients, and team members in business interactions.
10. Humorous: Uses levity to engage business associates and alleviate tension in high-stress situations.
11. Socratic: Uses questioning to stimulate critical business thinking and problem-solving.
12. Constructive: Offers feedback aimed at business growth and performance improvement.
13. Optimistic: Maintains a positive outlook on business prospects and potential success.
14. Realistic: Offers a practical and grounded perspective in business planning and expectations.
15. Encouraging: Boosts morale and confidence within entrepreneurial endeavors.
16. Appreciative: Recognizes and values the efforts and achievements of team members and business partners.
17. Reassuring: Alleviates concerns in business dealings, instilling confidence among stakeholders.
18. Inquisitive: Promotes exploration and curiosity in discovering new business opportunities and solutions.
19. Persuasive: Effectively convinces and influences stakeholders and clients towards beneficial business decisions.
20. Resilient: Exhibits toughness and adaptability in overcoming business challenges and adversities.
21. Visionary: Focuses on long-term business goals and innovative future strategies.
22. Energizing: Infuses enthusiasm and vigor into business teams and projects.
23. Compassionate: Demonstrates empathy and understanding in customer and client relations.
24. Professional: Upholds a formal and respectful demeanor in all business interactions.
25. Mindful: Shows awareness and consideration of the broader impact of business decisions on society and the environment.
26. Collaborative: Encourages teamwork and partnership in business ventures.
27. Dynamic: Adapts quickly to changing market trends and business environments.
28. Inspirational: Provokes higher aspirations and encourages big-picture thinking in business strategies.
29. Directive: Provides clear, actionable guidance crucial for timely business decisions and actions.
30. Resourceful: Demonstrates the ability to creatively utilize available resources for maximum business benefit.

Appendix No 6
Writing Styles for Business and Entrepreneurial Success

Writing style in business and entrepreneurial endeavors is pivotal for conveying ideas effectively, engaging stakeholders, and facilitating decision-making processes. Different styles can be leveraged to suit various business contexts, from presenting data to storytelling for brand building.

1. **Expository:** Clearly explains facts and information, ideal for business reports and data presentations.
2. **Descriptive:** Paints vivid pictures of products, services, or market scenarios, enhancing marketing materials.
3. **Narrative:** Tells stories, often used in brand storytelling or sharing entrepreneurial journeys.
4. **Persuasive:** Argues a point, crucial in sales pitches, proposals, or convincing stakeholders.
5. **Concise:** Delivers business communications or summaries in a brief, direct manner.
6. **Analytical:** Dissects business data or trends to convey underlying principles, useful in market analysis.
7. **Reflective:** Encourages introspection on past business decisions or experiences for learning.
8. **Dialogic:** Engages in a two-way conversation, useful for customer interactions or feedback sessions.
9. **Illustrative:** Uses real-world examples or case studies to clarify business strategies or concepts.
10. **Instructive:** Provides detailed business strategies, plans, or guidelines.
11. **Interpretive:** Explains complex business models or market dynamics.
12. **Comparative:** Analyzes competitors or different market strategies.
13. **Argumentative:** Defends business strategies or decisions, often seen in stakeholder meetings.
14. **Problem-Solution:** Identifies business challenges and proposes viable solutions.
15. **Evaluative:** Assesses the effectiveness of business strategies or marketing campaigns.
16. **Journalistic:** Reports business news or developments in an objective manner.
17. **Exploratory:** Explores new business ideas or market trends for innovative insights.
18. **Contemplative:** Encourages deep thought on future business directions or ethical considerations.

19. **Case Study:** Examines specific business scenarios or success stories for lessons.
20. **Research-based:** Utilizes empirical data and market research in business planning.
21. **Informal:** Adopts a casual style for internal communications or creative brainstorming.
22. **Formal:** Maintains professionalism in official business documents or communications.
23. **Technical:** Employs specialized business or industry terminology.
24. **Conceptual:** Explores high-level business ideas or models.
25. **Practical:** Focuses on actionable advice for immediate business application.
26. **Empirical:** Draws on real-world business experiences or observations.
27. **Theoretical:** Investigates theoretical business models or strategies.
28. **Storyboard:** Structures marketing or brand narratives in a sequenced manner.
29. **Interactive:** Engages the audience or stakeholders actively in business proposals or presentations.
30. **Scenario-based:** Outlines hypothetical business situations for strategic planning or training.

Appendix No 7
How to use ChatGPT to Draft Email Responses Faster

In today's fast-paced professional environment, efficient communication is key. A 2023 study by Slack and OnePoll highlights that American and British professionals spend approximately 11 hours weekly drafting around 112 emails. This equates to an average of 5 minutes per email, a significant time investment given the volume of correspondence.

ChatGPT is a transformative tool capable of drafting emails within seconds, offering a substantial time-saving advantage. The process is straightforward and accessible to you.

You can use the following **prompt**:

> *Draft a concise yet professional email saying that [INSERT WHAT YOU WANT TO COMMUNICATE OR SAY]. Keep it under 200 words.*

Consider the scenario of a real estate professional responding to a potential client's inquiry about commercial real estate investment opportunities. The executive might use the following prompt:

> *Draft a concise yet professional reply to this inquiry about commercial real estate opportunities, keeping it under 150 words.*

ChatGPT would then generate a professional and succinct reply, which could be further refined to better reflect the professional's voice or the specific context of the relationship, completing the process in under a minute.

Step-by-Step Guide to Drafting Email Replies with ChatGPT:

1. **Initiate ChatGPT:** Launch the ChatGPT application.
2. **Input Details:** Copy-paste the received email and articulate your intended response into the provided prompt structure.

3. **Review and Personalize:** Assess the response from ChatGPT, making any necessary adjustments to ensure it aligns with your tone and requirements before sending.

Transforming Email Replies During a Walk:

One innovative approach to managing email correspondence is utilizing ChatGPT while on a walk. This method not only promotes physical activity but also harnesses the creative benefits of walking to enhance communication effectiveness.

Procedure:

1. **Preparation:** Dress appropriately for a walk, ensuring you have your phone, headphones, and the necessary apps (ChatGPT and Gmail).
2. **Review Emails:** Glance through your inbox to identify emails requiring responses.
3. **Dictate Prompts:** Use the ChatGPT app to verbally dictate the essence of your desired email. ChatGPT is adept at understanding and organizing even the most casual or disjointed instructions into coherent drafts.
4. **Obtain Draft:** Submit your dictated prompt to ChatGPT to receive a drafted email.
5. **Edit and Send:** Make any tweaks to the draft to ensure it meets your standards and send it off.
6. **Repeat:** Continue this process for all pending emails.

This approach not only facilitates efficient email management but also integrates physical activity into your routine, enhancing overall productivity and well-being.

Expanding Creative Tasks: The versatility of ChatGPT extends beyond email drafting. For any creative task, you can record your thoughts or ideas and prompt ChatGPT to refine and structure them, leveraging its capability to transform raw ideas into polished outputs.

In summary, ChatGPT offers a revolutionary shift in managing professional correspondence, providing a time-efficient and flexible solution for drafting emails and other creative tasks.

Appendix No 8
How to Use AI Writing Tools to Draft Anything 2X Faster

Leveraging AI writing tools like ChatGPT can significantly expedite the drafting process, transforming how you could approach writing tasks. The key to maximizing these tools lies in a structured approach to crafting prompts, ensuring consistent and high-quality outputs.

The **WISER** framework, detailed below, serves as a comprehensive guide to achieving this goal.

WISER Framework Overview:

- **W (Who):** Establish context by assigning ChatGPT a role or identity that suits your writing task. This sets the tone and perspective for the draft. Here is an example of a prompt:

Pretend you're a marketing expert familiar with tech audiences interested in CRM tools.

- **I (Instructions):** Clearly articulate the task at hand with explicit instructions, ensuring ChatGPT understands exactly what is required. Here is an example of a prompt:

  Compose a 300-word article for small business owners highlighting how CRM software addresses their common challenges.

- **S (Subtasks):** Break down the main task into smaller, manageable components, guiding ChatGPT through each step of the drafting process. Here is an example of a prompt:

  Start by defining CRM software, discuss its benefits for small businesses, and conclude with an invitation to try a new tool. Then, re-read the output and iterate one more time to make it even more persuasive and concise.

- **E (Examples):** Provide specific examples or templates to help ChatGPT align its output with your desired style or content. Here is an example of a prompt:

  Refer to the following example of a blog post effectively showcasing project management tools' advantages for small businesses: <insert example here>

- **R (Review):** Critically evaluate the initial draft you get from ChatGPT. Use the feedback loop to refine the content in terms of tone, length, or depth. Here is an example of a prompt:

  Write another version of the above blog post, now with the perspective from a successful entrepreneur, adjusting the tone and writing style accordingly. Subsequently, provide 10 alternative titles.

Implementing the WISER Framework:

To employ the WISER framework effectively, clarity and specificity in your prompts are crucial. The detailed template provided below can be customized to fit various writing projects. Simply fill in the [PLACEHOLDERS] according to the instructions.

You are a [IDENTITY]. Please write a [INSERT WHAT YOU WANT TO WRITE] as a [DEFINE THE IDENTITY OR ENVIRONMENT]. The goal is to [INSERT GOAL].

Instructions:

[INSERT DETAILED INSTRUCTIONS FOR WHAT YOU WANT]

Here is the process I would like you to use:

In case you are not happy with the output from ChatGPT, you can proceed with the following prompt for the review:

To refine your drafts, consider using ChatGPT for this too. ChatGPT offers feedback and revision suggestions, acting as a versatile editing assistant to polish your document. Consider the following prompt:

Appendix No 9
Strategic Phrasing for Enhancing your Prompts

Insert the following phrases into your prompts for enhanced responses from ChatGPT.

Inspiring Creativity:
- Explore unconventional solutions and alternative perspectives.
- Unearth hidden gems and non-traditional methods.
- Delve into uncharted territories and groundbreaking concepts.
- Investigate unexpected avenues and creative pathways.
- Suggest fresh approaches and inventive strategies.

Ensuring Thoroughness and Quality:
- Provide an exhaustive and all-encompassing analysis.
- Deliver a rigorous and thoroughgoing examination.
- Create a systematic and far-reaching overview.
- Furnish a complete and unreserved understanding.
- Render an in-depth and wide-spectrum exploration.

Highlighting Specificity:
- Emphasize untapped potentials and overlooked facets.

- Accentuate neglected dimensions and underexplored horizons.
- Focus on disregarded elements and obscured opportunities.
- Underline unnoticed details and hidden prospects.
- Illuminate obscure paths and unattended aspects.

Enhancing Engagement:
- Share tailored guidance and personalized insights.
- Offer specialized recommendations and industry-specific advice.
- Suggest actionable strategies and practical solutions.
- Convey targeted wisdom and sector-focused guidance.
- Present relevant examples and context-specific ideas.

Others:
- Include uncommon advice and underrated resources.
- Provide unique insights and overlooked opportunities.
- Share distinctive guidance and unexplored options.
- Provide a meticulous and wide-ranging response.
- Impart unconventional wisdom and under-the-radar tools.

Appendix No 10
GPTs for Business Success

To access these GPTs, search for their names in the GPTs store, visit the provided links, or scan the QR codes.

1. **Business Ideas Generator Advisor GPT:**

    https://chat.openai.com/g/g-xvfviP7xD-business-ideas-generator-advisor

Turn ideas into profit with ChatGPT! Discover lucrative business ventures tailored for you.

By Mauricio Vasquez

2. Digital Marketing and Sales Advisor GPT:
https://chat.openai.com/g/g-K5Y5xBwC0-digital-marketing-and-sales-advisor

3. Financial Planning and Analysis Strategist GPT:
https://chat.openai.com/g/g-OW77NMkIv-financial-planning-and-analysis-strategist

4. E-commerce and Online Business Mentor GPT:
https://chat.openai.com/g/g-nMlroYOh7-e-commerce-and-online-business-mentor

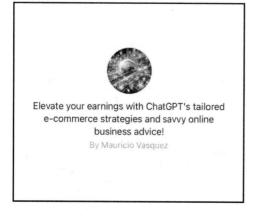

5. Freelancing and Remote Work Coach GPT:

https://chat.openai.com/g/g-ODjpvyNMY-freelancing-and-remote-work-coach

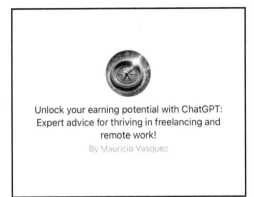

6. Startup and Entrepreneurship Strategist GPT:

https://chat.openai.com/g/g-wmGjEwhvy-startup-and-entrepreneurship-strategist

7. Productivity and Time Management Counselor GPT:

https://chat.openai.com/g/g-alCoCP33s-productivity-and-time-management-counselor

8. Digital Wall Art Creator AI GPT:

https://chat.openai.com/g/g-QqoggNJhF-digital-wall-art-creator-ai

9. Optimus Text-to-Text Prompt Engineering Tutor GPT:

https://chat.openai.com/g/g-GbYHlUyyJ-optimus-text-to-text-prompt-engineering-tutor

10. Book Creation Assistant AI GPT:

https://chat.openai.com/g/g-vqxrHcJZR-book-creation-assistant-ai

11. Business and Entrepreneurship Coach AI GPT:

https://chat.openai.com/g/g-GL5pdNgqh-business-and-entrepreneurship-coach-ai

Guides on idea validation, strategic planning,
growth strategies, financial management,
marketing, leadership, operational efficiency,
and legal guidance in business.

By Mauricio Vasquez

12. Etssy Online Marketplace Expert GPT

https://chat.openai.com/g/g-kPCeQKcK9-etssy-online-marketplace-expert

Expert in Etsy setup, SEO, marketing,
branding, and customer engagement
strategies.

By Mauricio Vasquez

13. Custom Instructions Producer GPT

https://chat.openai.com/g/g-lJeuWgZxl-custom-instructions-producer

Help users to set their ChatGPT Customs
Instructions by responding to: (1) What would
you like ChatGPT to know about you to
provide better responses?, & (2) How would
you like ChatGPT to respond?

By Mauricio Vasquez

Appendix No 11
About the Author

Mauricio Vasquez is a multifaceted professional with over 20 years of experience in risk management and insurance, specializing in sectors like mining, power, and renewable energy. He holds an Industrial Engineering degree, a Master's in Business Administration, and a Master's in Marketing and Commercial Management, along with certifications in Enterprise Risk Management and Artificial Intelligence.

Mauricio is also a certified Adler Trained Coach and a self-published author, focusing on personal growth and professional development. His expertise in Artificial Intelligence and Large Language Models Prompt engineering adds a unique layer to his professional background.

Fluent in both English and Spanish, Mauricio has worked across Canada, the U.S., Latin America, and the Caribbean. In addition to his corporate roles, he is a Professional and Life Coach, committed to helping immigrants transition successfully to new lives in Canada. His approach is deeply rooted in building long-term relationships and providing tailored, impactful solutions to clients.

Unlock the full potential of prompt engineering with ChatGPT through exclusive 1-on-1 coaching sessions tailored just for you. As a reader of this book, you're entitled to an extraordinary offer: enjoy a 25% discount on your personalized guidance journey. Use your promo code: "PROMOCODE25%". Connect with Mauricio through LinkedIn to schedule your session.

Don't miss this opportunity to elevate your skills with expert insights. Reach out now and begin transforming your understanding of ChatGPT.

If you want to connect with Mauricio, go to this link https://www.linkedin.com/in/mauriciovasquez or scan this QR code:

www.ingramcontent.com/pod-product-compliance
Lightning Source LLC
LaVergne TN
LVHW082033050326
832904LV00006B/277